50 Walks in

SOMERSET

D1514331

First published 2002
Researched and written by Ronald Turnbull

Produced by AA Publishing
© Automobile Association Developments Limited 2002
Illustrations © Automobile Association Developments Limited 2002
Reprinted 2004 (twice)

All rights reserved. No part of this publication may be reproduced, stored in a
retrieval system, or transmitted in any form or by any means – electronic,
photocopying, recording or otherwise – unless the written permission of the
publishers has been obtained beforehand.

Published by AA Publishing (a trading name of Automobile Association
Developments Limited, whose registered office is Millstream, Maidenhead
Road, Windsor, SL4 5GD;
registered number 1878835).

O S Ordnance Survey® This product includes mapping data licensed from
Ordnance Survey® with the permission of the Controller
of Her Majesty's Stationery Office.
© Crown copyright 2004. All rights reserved. Licence number 399221

ISBN 0 7495 3331 5

A CIP catalogue record for this book is available
from the British Library.

The contents of this book are believed correct at the time of printing.
Nevertheless, the publishers cannot be held responsible for any errors or
omissions or for changes in the details given in this book or for the
consequences of any reliance on the information it provides. This does not
affect your statutory rights. We have tried to ensure accuracy in this book, but
things do change and we would be grateful if readers would advise us of any
inaccuracies they may encounter.

We have taken all reasonable steps to ensure that these walks are
safe and achievable by walkers with a realistic level of fitness.
However, all outdoor activities involve a degree of risk and the publishers
accept no responsibility for any injuries caused to
readers whilst following these walks. For more advice on walking safely see
page 128. The mileage range shown on the front cover is for guidance only –
some walks may exceed or be less than these distances.

Visit the AA Publishing website at www.theAA.com

Paste-up and editorial by Outcrop Publishing Services Ltd, Cumbria
for AA Publishing

A02237

Printed in Italy by G Canale & C SPA, Torino, Italy

Legend

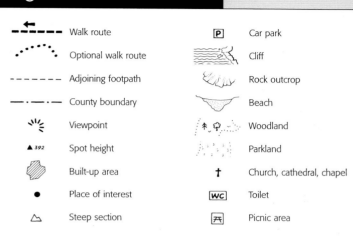

◄-------	Walk route	P	Car park
·······•	Optional walk route	≈≈≈	Cliff
-------	Adjoining footpath		Rock outcrop
—·—·—	County boundary		Beach
☼	Viewpoint	♠ ♣	Woodland
▲ 392	Spot height		Parkland
	Built-up area	†	Church, cathedral, chapel
●	Place of interest	WC	Toilet
△	Steep section	ㅈ	Picnic area

Somerset locator map

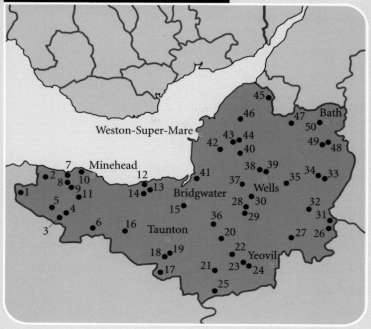

Contents

Rating: Each walk is rated for its relative difficulty compared to the other walks in this book. Walks marked 🚶🚶 🚶 🚶 are likely to be shorter and easier with little total ascent. The hardest walks are marked 🚶🚶 🚶🚶 🚶🚶 .

Walking in Safety: For advice and safety tips ➤ 128.

Contents

Introducing Somerset

In ancient Greek mythology, when Zeus sent two eagles to fly inwards from the ends of the Earth he discovered that the centre of everything was at the sacred oracle of Delphi. Today, in Somerset, he'd have to use buzzards: one bird would start at the Avon Gorge, soaring across the wide, traffic-noisy space below the Clifton Bridge; the other would rise out of an ancient oak by Badgworthy Water or, as it is better known, 'Doone Valley'. You don't need a ruler to work out that the two would meet at Glastonbury. Alighting on the top of Glastonbury Tor, they would look down on the town that stretches across time as effortlessly as our two birds stretch across space – from ancient through medieval to modern.

Somerset's towns of golden limestone, tile and thatch are the first part of what the county's all about. Looking outwards, our birds next observe the bumpy nature of the surroundings: Somerset may not be high, but it is hilly. In the far west a brown line along the horizon is the edge of Exmoor – more than half of the National Park is in our county,

including its highest point at Dunkery Beacon. Slightly closer come the Brendons and the Blackdowns: rounded, friendly hills, criss-crossed with little lanes. To the south are the 'Green Hills of Somerset', famous enough to have their own song, and finished off on top with an Iron Age fort. Then there are the Mendips and the Quantocks: small but splendid limestone, covered with rabbit-nibbled meadow and wild flowers. Apologies here to Yorkshire: the finest limestone scenery, the best of the crags and gorges, is here among the Mendips. Closest of all are the tiny Poldens, their steep sides clothed with woodland and one proud outcrop of crag. By my count Somerset has seven hill ranges – that's one more than the whole of Snowdonia…

Admittedly Snowdonia's hills are bigger, but when you look out from Snowdon all you get is a narrow valley and another hill on the other side. Look out from a Somerset hill and you see a patchwork of bright fields. At sunset, from Glastonbury Tor, those fields have a green glow that's almost like dragon skin. Every few miles there rises another of Somerset's golden-orange church towers, and a silver river winds into the distance.

These rivers bring us to Somerset's most special sort of country. Elsewhere in England there are flat lands – Lincolnshire, Norfolk, the Cambridgeshire Fens – and flat they certainly are, but only from the Somerset Levels do you look up to the hills; and from the hills you look down over the Levels. A typical Somerset walk might be a wander

---

PUBLIC TRANSPORT   ⓘ

Somerset has an efficient network of railways and bus routes. The steam-hauled West Somerset Railway (from Bishops Lydeard, near Taunton, to Minehead) and Wessex Trains' line from Bristol to Weymouth can be used to create fine cross-country walks. A set of five timetable booklets (free) covers the county; they are stocked in post offices as well as tourist information centres. Any one route may have multiple operators – check your proposed journey.

through the reclaimed wetlands, among butterflies and reed beds, followed by a hill that could be as tiny as Burrow Mump (100ft/30m) for a wide view back across it all. With hilltops at the top, and the Levels at the bottom, that still leaves the hillsides. Somerset hillsides are surprisingly steep – there's a reason for this, involving the basically horizontal geology. They are also surprisingly green. Hillside woodlands, many of them of ancient oak or beech, grow dense and bushy. Thus another typical walk might follow a little stream, running up inside a big wood, and an open, airy hilltop above it all.

But then there are the stone-built towns to admire, the limestone gorges to marvel at, the legendary footprints of Kings Arthur and Alfred to retrace; there are the Doones to be done, and the literary walking of Samuel Taylor Coleridge; there's even some Somerset shoreline.

All this diversity awaits you, but it is better not to be one of Zeus's buzzards. Somerset is no place for a quick fly-by, it's a county for walking.

Using this Book

Information panels
An information panel for each walk shows its relative difficulty (➤ 5), the distance and total amount of ascent. An indication of the gradients you will encounter is shown by the rating ▲▲ ▲▲ ▲▲ (no steep slopes) to ▲▲ ▲▲ ▲▲ (several very steep slopes).

Maps
There are 30 maps, covering 40 of the walks. Some walks have a suggested option in the same area. The information panel for these walks will tell you how much extra walking is involved. On short-cut suggestions the panel will tell you the total distance if you set out from the start of the main walk. Where an option returns to the same point on the main walk, just the distance of the loop is given. Where an option leaves the main walk at one point and returns to it at another, then the distance shown is for the whole walk. The minimum time suggested is for reasonably fit walkers and doesn't allow for stops. Each walk has a suggested map. Laminated aqua3 maps are longer lasting and water resistant.

Start Points
The start of each walk is given as a six-figure grid reference prefixed by two letters indicating which 100km square of the National Grid it refers to. You'll find more information on grid references on most Ordnance Survey maps.

Dogs
We have tried to give dog owners useful advice about how dog friendly each walk is. Please respect other countryside users. Keep your dog under control, especially around livestock, and obey local bylaws and other dog control notices.

Car Parking
Many of the car parks suggested are public, but occasionally you may find you have to park on the roadside or in a lay-by. Please be considerate when you leave your car, ensuring that access roads or gates are not blocked and that other vehicles can pass safely.

Walk 1

Pinkery Pond to Moles Chamber

Experience quintessential Exmoor among the barrows and tumuli of its Bronze-Age farmers.

•DISTANCE•	5¾ miles (9.2km)
•MINIMUM TIME•	3hrs
•ASCENT / GRADIENT•	700ft (210m) ▲▲▲
•LEVEL OF DIFFICULTY•	林 林 林
•PATHS•	Narrow moorland paths following fences and some tracks, 4 stiles
•LANDSCAPE•	Bleak, grassy moorland
•SUGGESTED MAP•	aqua3 OS Outdoor Leisure 9 Exmoor
•START / FINISH•	Grid reference: SS 728401
•DOG FRIENDLINESS•	Be aware of possible livestock, ponies and deer on open moorland
•PARKING•	Unmarked roadside pull-off on B3358 on Chains Hill
•PUBLIC TOILETS•	None on route; nearest in Simonsbath car park

BACKGROUND TO THE WALK

Chains Barrow is the highest point on the waterlogged Exmoor plateau of purple moor grass and deer sedge. Other walks hereabouts are Exmoor more or less; this one is Exmoor pure and simple. It has views out to the sea and to the sheltered lands below. It's a walk for a sunny day with skylarks, or for a chill one in autumn. In cloud and rain, with the bog at full squelch, you absorb a lot of atmosphere (and quite a bit of the rain), though this may not be everyone's idea of fun.

Bronze Age Exmoor

In about 2000 BC the hunter-gatherer lifestyle of the Stone Age came to an end on Exmoor. In the Bronze Age that followed we find traces of agriculture, with crops, such as barley, and livestock (mostly cattle and sheep). We also find the round barrows, for example, Chains Barrow and Longstone Barrow, scattered across the moorland summits. Elsewhere in Somerset the standing stones are of the Bronze Age – charred wood accidentally buried under the stones can be carbon-dated. More doubtfully, Tarr Steps in the south of Exmoor are also credited to the Bronze-Age people (► Walk 3).

It used to be thought that the change from the Stone Age to the Bronze Age came about by conquest: better swords and axes allowed the new people to kill or enslave the old. Today, tree pollen preserved in peat bogs can be dated very accurately, and shows that the clearance of the moors for farming was a gradual process. The scratch-plough was perhaps more important than the sword: experts believe that it was the idea of sitting still and starting a farm that conquered, rather than a particular tribe. The climate was warmer and drier in those days, and the moorland was grass rather than peat. Large areas will have been hedged and banked for pasture: on Dartmoor, 25,000 acres (10,000ha) of Bronze Age-enclosures have been mapped out.

High Society

The shepherds belonged to a wider social unit than the family or farmstead. At least some of the people in charge had enough importance to build up collections of 50 or 60 axe heads, implying that the Bronze Age farmers weren't entirely peaceful people. Someone else had enough spare time to build the long barrows and raise the standing stones, and there were jewellers working in jadeite and bronze.

It isn't known why the people of the Bronze Age chose to build their barrows here on the bleakest of hilltops. Perhaps they were scared of the spirits of the dead and wanted to keep them out of the way, or perhaps a really large, conspicuous barrow would intimidate the people on the next hill.

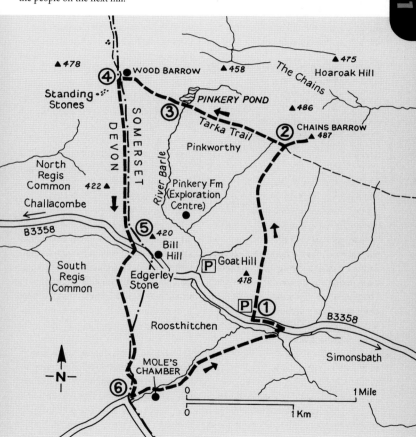

Walk 1 **Directions**

① At the **Simonsbath** end of the pull-off is a gate with a bridleway sign for **Chains Barrow**. Go up the right-hand edges of two fields, then head 35yds (32m) left, to a gate.

The way across the following rough moorland is marked by occasional yellow-topped posts. Go gently uphill, parallel with a hedge away on the left. The marked way bends slightly right, up the crest of a wide moorland spur. At the top is a bank with a gateway.

Walk 1

② A signpost indicates a sketchy path out over the moor to **Chains Barrow**. Return to the gateway and follow the fenced bank. It leads across the moor top to **Pinkery Pond**; this is crossed on its dam.

③ Follow the fence as it continues uphill to a corner of access land. Maintain your direction across moorland for 350yds (320m) to join a high bank, and follow this to the left, to **Wood Barrow**.

WHILE YOU'RE THERE ⓘ
The **Exmoor Steam Railway** runs steam trains along a mile (1.6km) of narrow gauge track above Bratton Fleming. It's England's highest narrow gauge railway, with wide views over the valley of the Devon Yeo.

④ The gate ahead leads into Devonshire. Beyond, Wood Barrow is one of many put to more conventional use, originally by the Saxons, as markers of the Devon boundary. In front of **Woodbarrow Gate** turn left on a signed bridleway track, with a high bank on its right. This leads off the moor. Bear left around a sheep-pen made of disused metal crash barriers. A gate leads on to the **B3358**.

WHAT TO LOOK FOR ⓘ
From Wood Barrow, at the top of this walk, the land to the west is an access area under the Country Stewardship Scheme. Here, skilled map readers can go adventuring across the moor in search of **Longstone Barrow**, and the Long Stone itself, a standing stone 9ft (3m) high, raised during the Bronze Age.

⑤ Cross into a track signposted 'Mole's Chamber'. This climbs for ¼ mile (400m) to a signpost. Here you must bear left across featureless moorland for 550yds (503m). A field corner soon comes into sight: on the right is high banking with a fence in front, and on the left is lower banking with a fence on top; between these two is the destination gate. Go straight downhill to a stream, with a peaty track starting beyond it. Follow this up and then bending right, to reach the end of a tarred road.

⑥ Turn left, away from the road. A faint old track runs down across a stream to a narrow gate with a blue paint-spot. An improving path runs down to the right of the stream, gradually slanting up to a gate. Here join a larger track, but immediately after the gate keep ahead as the larger track bends right. A faint green track runs parallel with the river down on the left, to reach a signposted gate. Turn left on a tarred track, to join the **B3358**. Turn left to the parking pull-off.

WHERE TO EAT AND DRINK ⓘ
The **Exmoor Forest Hotel** at Simonsbath serves good food and Exmoor Ale (brewed in Wiveliscombe, ► Walk 16), but no lunches in winter. Dogs are welcome. The bar is decorated with bits of dead animals. Indeed, this is your best chance of sighting a badger: there's a stuffed one climbing the wall above the fireplace.

Down the Doone Valley

Fact and fiction intertwine in this moorland valley walk which visits the tiny church celebrated in R D Blackmore's classic novel.

•DISTANCE•	8¾ miles (14.1km)
•MINIMUM TIME•	4hrs 30min
•ASCENT / GRADIENT•	1,250ft (380m) ▲▲▲
•LEVEL OF DIFFICULTY•	🚶🚶 🚶🚶 🚶
•PATHS•	Some steep ascents and descents, pathless open moor, 1 stile
•LANDSCAPE•	Bleak, grassy moor, then a charming enclosed valley
•SUGGESTED MAP•	aqua3 OS Outdoor Leisure 9 Exmoor
•START / FINISH•	Grid reference: SS 820464
•DOG FRIENDLINESS•	Well-controlled – livestock throughout, horse riders in Doone Valley
•PARKING•	Car park (free) at Robbers Bridge
•PUBLIC TOILETS•	None on route; toilets at County Gate on A39

BACKGROUND TO THE WALK

It's not often that a place invented in a story gets mapped in black print by the Ordnance Survey. But the area of Exmoor where Somerset and Devon meet is marked on the Outdoor Leisure map as 'Doone Country'; and the paths leading towards Badgworthy Water are all signposted 'Doone Valley'.

R D Blackmore

Near the foot of the valley is a monument to the man responsible, Richard Dodderidge Blackmore (1825–1900), 'whose novel *Lorna Doone* extols to all the world the joys of Exmoor'. Badgworthy Water is not really Doone Valley. There's no point in trying to work out which window of Oare church is the one Carver pointed his carbine through to shoot Lorna on her wedding day – Carver never existed, so didn't need a window.

Mythical Crags

In some strange way Blackmore's Exmoor is more real and romantic than the flat Exmoor of fact. The angle at the top of the Badgworthy (grid ref SS 795434) really is Doone Gate, defended with a barrier and a tunnel – here Jan Ridd and Jeremy Stickles made their disastrous assault in Chapter 54. Walking down the valley, we mentally move the medieval village into the main valley, and place the small house of the sinister Counsellor Doone across the stream itself. At the same time we must raise the valley walls higher, and add rocks and crags to the slopes of heather, hawthorn and gorse that we see in the real world.

As for the enclosed and dangerous waterslide that Jan Ridd clambers up to meet his Lorna, that won't be found at all, unless it's in the side valley of Lank Combe. Exmoor has bogs, but none of them is the Wizard's Slough, deep enough to swallow up the mighty Carver Doone. And there are no gold mines. It's at Oare church that romance and reality come together, for the building is virtually as it is in Blackmore's book, and one John Ridd was churchwarden there no longer ago than 1925.

The Doones of Badgworthy

The Doones of Badgworthy existed in local legend before *Lorna Doone*, certainly as a story to scare naughty children, and possibly in fact. Lawless men did take refuge on Exmoor in the aftermath of the Civil War and the Monmouth Rebellion. However, they could scarcely have plundered the countryside and murdered its inhabitants for a full century without ever appearing in the law court records of the time.

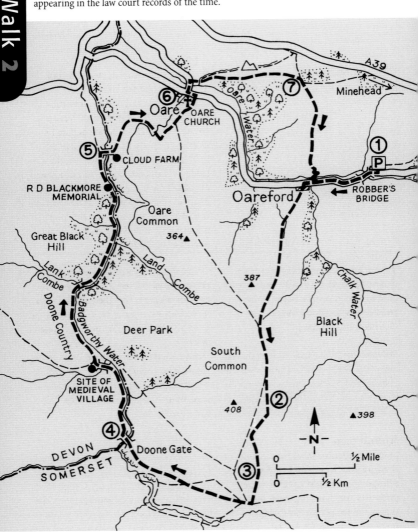

Walk 2 Directions

① Cross **Robber's Bridge** and follow the road to **Oareford**. Turn left on the bridleway signed

'Larkbarrow'. After a mile (1.6km), at a gate on to open moor with only a faint track continuing ahead, bear left. Follow a fence, continuing over the moorland crest to the corner of the large field.

Walk 2

WHAT TO LOOK FOR ⓘ
The outlines of the former **Badgworthy village** are clearly visible above the foot of Hoccombe Combe. The buildings are the two-room long house, with cattle on one side and people on the other. The last inhabitant, a shepherd, is said to have died in a blizzard with his little granddaughter around the year 1800.

② Go through a gate on the left, then a narrow gate on the right on to rougher moorland. Take a green path ahead for 140yds (128m). Here bear slightly right on a smaller path to go through a shallow col or gap. Now a much wider path arrives from the right. Bear left to a gate in a bank marking the edge of an **Exmoor Park Access Area**.

③ The path ahead leads down, with a bank on its left, to a signpost. Turn right ('**Doone Valley**') on a clear path that gradually climbs to a gate in the Access Area bank – it runs down to a footbridge over **Badgworthy Water**.

WHERE TO EAT AND DRINK ⓘ
There are convenient tea rooms at **Cloud Farm**, near the end of the route, and just above where the waterslide in Chapter 7 of *Lorna Doone* would be (if it existed).

④ Turn right, downstream. After a plank footbridge a gate leads into the hummocks of the lost **medieval village**. Go straight up to a wide path and turn right. Continue down the valley to a large footbridge leading across to **Cloud Farm**.

⑤ Pass to the left of **Cloud Farm**, on to a track that passes through a farm shed, then climbs out of the valley. Where it ends, follow the lower side of a field to the edge of a little wooded combe. Turn right for 70yds (64m) to a gate on the left. A track passes above the combe and turns down beyond it. Where the track bends right, keep straight downhill through waymarked gates, to turn left on the valley road below beside **Oare church**.

⑥ Turn right, signposted 'Porlock', and follow the road for 130yds (118m) to cross **Oare Water**. Turn right along the riverside to cross a small stream (there's no footbridge, although one is marked on the OS map). A few paces further on, turn up left to a small, abandoned house and then turn right between gorse bushes. A grass path leads straight up a sharp spur. It continues beside a fence to a stile; keep ahead, across heather, to a plantation.

⑦ Turn right along a track, and at the plantation's corner keep ahead on a smaller track ('Oareford'). This bends left near a field corner; here keep ahead on a path towards some tall trees. Pass to the right of these trees, which mark ancient field edges, to a small gate. A path leads steeply down to a footbridge into **Oareford**. Turn left to return to your car.

WHILE YOU'RE THERE ⓘ
Oare church needed no added romance from R D Blackmore, even if he did have to put in an extra window. In 800 years of extensions, decorations and repairs, nothing ugly has found its way into this tiny church. The eye travels happily from the Norman font to the buzzard lectern, carved as recently as 1999. Among many small treasures, I particularly like the cherubic memorials of 1772 and 1791.

Walk 3

A Round of Applause for Tarr Steps

Visit one of the 'oldest' bridges in the world, set in a quiet valley clothed in ancient woodland.

•DISTANCE•	5¼ miles (8.4km)
•MINIMUM TIME•	2hrs 30min
•ASCENT / GRADIENT•	700ft (210m) ▲▲ ▲▲ ▲
•LEVEL OF DIFFICULTY•	👥 👥 👥
•PATHS•	Riverside paths and field tracks, some open moor, no stiles
•LANDSCAPE•	Wooded river valley and pasture slopes above
•SUGGESTED MAP•	aqua3 OS Outdoor Leisure 9 Exmoor
•START / FINISH•	Grid reference: SS 872323
•DOG FRIENDLINESS•	Dogs can run off-lead along River Barle
•PARKING•	Just over ¼ mile (400m) east of Tarr Steps – can be full in summer. (Parking at Tarr Steps for disabled people only)
•PUBLIC TOILETS•	At car park

BACKGROUND TO THE WALK

This is the longest and best clapper stone bridge in Britain; as such it featured on a postage stamp in 1968. (The others in the set were the stone military bridge at Aberfeldy; Telford's Menai Bridge; and a concrete viaduct on the M4.) Bronze-Age trackways converge on to this river crossing, suggesting that the bridge itself may be about 4,000 years old. Given that it gets swept away and rebuilt after every major flood, this date for its construction is pure guesswork – or, to use the archaeological term, 'conjectural'. It is still arguably Europe's oldest bridge.

'Cleaca' Bridge

The name 'clapper' probably comes from the Saxon 'cleaca', meaning stepping stones. The first clapper bridges arose as stone slabs laid across the top of existing stepping stones. With a serviceable ford alongside, this one is clearly a luxury rather than a necessity. It's only because the local sedimentary rocks form such suitable slabs that it was built at all. At 59yds (54m), Tarr Steps is by far the longest of the 40 or so clapper bridges left in Britain.

Right of Way

As the bridge is a public highway you could, in theory, be entitled to ride your bicycle across it. (I have seen this done, though not tried it myself.) Quite clearly, the damage you might do to yourself by falling off the bridge could be very serious. That said, the feat is not as hard as it looks – the secret seems to lie in avoiding catching the front wheel in the slots where the bridge top consists of two separate, parallel stones. The ford alongside is popular with horse riders and canoeists, though the Highway Code does not seem to specify who gives way when the one meets the other. It's always very pleasing to see these three non-motorised forms of transport in action together, while motorists are unable to make it down the congested narrow road.

The Woods

Local legend gives the bridge a devilish origin. Apparently Satan himself built it for sunbathing on. The shady groves of ancient woodland, that drove him into the middle of the river, form probably the best birdwatching terrain in the country – you need only to sit or stand quietly in the shadow of a tree trunk and wait for the birds to parade before you. It's also good for the birds, offering them safety from hawks and buzzards, plenty of nest sites, insects to eat and open flight paths between the branches.

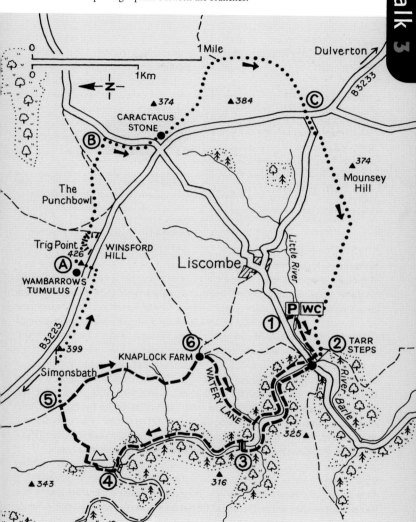

Walk 3 Directions

① Leave the bottom of the car park by a footpath on the left-hand side, signposted 'Scenic Path'. This takes you down to the left of the road to the **Little River**, crossing two footbridges on its way to **Tarr Steps**, over the River Barle, ahead.

Walk 3

② Cross the Steps, turning upstream at the far side (signposted 'Circular Walk'). Follow a wide riverbank path past what looks like an exciting wire footbridge but is, in fact, a device for intercepting floating trees in times of flood. After ¾ mile (1.2km) the path crosses a side-stream on stepping stones, and immediately afterwards reaches a long footbridge over the **River Barle**.

> **WHERE TO EAT AND DRINK** ⓘ
>
> If you didn't bring your own picnic, the tea rooms at **Tarr Farm** are ideally situated, just above the Steps. There are no pubs on the walk, but not too far away is the **Rock Inn** at Dulverton; others are at Winsford and Withypool.

> **WHAT TO LOOK FOR** ⓘ
>
> For non-specialists, some of the more easily recognised birds are: the dipper (small, black-and-white, bobs on a rock) grey wagtail (yellow underside, wags its tail) and the kingfisher (flash of blue passing up or down the river). The observant should spot the standing heron even before it unfolds itself like an umbrella and takes to the air.

③ Cross, and continue upstream, with the river now on the left. After ¾ mile (1.2km) the path crosses a small wooden footbridge, and then divides at a signpost.

④ Turn right, uphill, signed 'Winsford Hill'. A wide path goes up through the woods with a stream on its right. Where it meets a track turn briefly right to ford the stream, then continue uphill on a narrower signed path. At a low bank with beech trees turn right to a gate and follow the foot of a field to a tarred lane. Go up this to a cattle grid on to the open moor. Here, bear right on a faint track that heads up between gorse bushes. After 250yds (229m) it reaches a 4-way signpost.

⑤ Turn right ('Knaplock') and slant down to a hedge corner. Follow this hedge briefly, then take a path that slants gradually up into the moor. After 170yds (155m) a sign points back down towards the moor-foot banking. A beech bank crosses ahead: aim for the lower end of this, where a soft track leads forward, with occasional blue paint-spots. After ¼ mile (400m) the track turns downhill, then back to the left. It becomes firmer and drier as it reaches **Knaplock Farm**.

> **WHILE YOU'RE THERE** ⓘ
>
> The thatched village of **Winsford** is delightful in itself but poses a problem in mathematics: is it possible to walk over all of its seven bridges without passing over any of them twice?

⑥ Among the farm buildings turn downhill signed '**Tarr Steps**', on to a muddy farm track. Where this turns off into a field, continue ahead in a stony track, **Watery Lane**. After its initial descent this becomes a smooth path down to the **River Barle**. Turn left, downstream. When the path rises a little above the river, look out for a fork on the right, signed 'Footpath'. This rejoins the river to pass through an open field that's just right for a more comfortable sunbathe than the busy Tarr Steps downstream. Cross the road and turn left up the scenic path to return to your car.

Winsford Hill

For a longer walk around Tarr Steps take this higher option, above the wooded riverside, to join the ponies on the heathy hill.
See map and information panel for Walk 3

•DISTANCE•	7¾ miles (12.5km)
•MINIMUM TIME•	3hrs 45min
•ASCENT / GRADIENT•	1,000ft (300m) ▲▲▲
•LEVEL OF DIFFICULTY•	👫 👫 👫

Walk 4 Directions (Walk 3 option)

At Point ⑤ keep ahead, signed '**Winsford Hill**'. The green track slants up through gorse, thorn bushes, and some heather. With the railing of the B3223 road visible just above, fork right on to a track that runs gently uphill. This keeps parallel with the road and well below it. You may spot a quartz outcrop just below the track. At its highest point the track narrows between gorse bushes and, 100yds (91m) further on, a small path turns up to the left. This leads to the road: cross it to the trig point on **Winsford Hill**, Point Ⓐ.

Continue ahead, towards **Dunkery Hill** (which fills the northern horizon), for just a short way, to reach a corner of the fence which protects Wambarrows tumulus from feet and hooves. Turn right, on to a green track that runs gently downhill to the head of the deep **Punchbowl** hollow on the left. Here the main path bears slightly left and continues level – ignore smaller paths descending further to the left. Keep ahead over the crest of a gentle ridge, and down to the lane

(Point Ⓑ) that runs around the base of the open moorland.

The path continues immediately above the road, on its right. At a 'Give way' sign, cross the road to the shelter around the **Caractacus Stone**. The wide path continues just above the high hedge bank marking the foot of the moor. Where a track comes up out of the fields on the left, go straight across, and continue on the track round the moor foot. After another ½ mile (800m) the hedge bends left: here continue ahead to a signpost standing at a road junction, Point Ⓒ.

Cross on to a minor road, shortly leading to a cattle grid. Here keep ahead on a track between gateposts. After 100yds (91m) bear left at a sign for Tarr Steps, on to a rougher track. After a gate with a signpost the path bears slightly right, away from a hedge on the left. Opposite the start-point car park, ignore a horizontal cross-path but continue the gentle descent into birch woods. At the foot of the slope the path reaches a small gate and a leafy, sunken way down to the **River Barle**. Turn right for a few steps to **Tarr Steps**, and turn up to the right (before the footbridge) on to the scenic path.

Withypool's River and Common

A short walk up the wooded riverside and on to the grassy moorland.

•DISTANCE•	3½ miles (5.7km)
•MINIMUM TIME•	1hr 45min
•ASCENT / GRADIENT•	350ft (100m) ▲ ▲ ▲
•LEVEL OF DIFFICULTY•	👥 👥 👥
•PATHS•	Narrow riverside path, field paths and open moor, 15 stiles
•LANDSCAPE•	Small moorland valley
•SUGGESTED MAP•	aqua3 OS Outdoor Leisure 9 Exmoor
•START / FINISH•	Grid reference: SS 844354
•DOG FRIENDLINESS•	Appropriate control over fields, riverside and moorland
•PARKING•	Small car park (free, busy on summer weekends) just across river from Withypool village
•PUBLIC TOILETS•	In village centre, opposite shop

Walk 5 Directions

The upper Barle Valley is the heart of Exmoor: not dramatic combes and the sudden seaside, but a gentle and rather melancholy landscape. A small gate marked 'Picnic Place' leads out of the car park to the **River Barle**. Turn left, following the river bank upstream. Withycombe, with its wooded brook, lies below long grass slopes and the bare moorland plateau. The walk makes its way up the River Barle for about 1½ miles (2.4km), gradually working up through fields away from the stream. At the edge of moorland it turns back to return along the top of the enclosed lands.

> ### WHERE TO EAT AND DRINK ⓘ
> The **Royal Oak** has an 'Exmoor staghound' sort of atmosphere – authentic, but not necessarily attractive to today's visitor. Alternative food supplies are at the small shop, which is also a local information centre.

The bare moorland plateau is characterised by a quiet that may be disturbed by the occasional whinny of a pony. Ponies have been on Exmoor for longer than people: they are the closest there is to the original wild horse of Europe. A hundred years ago they came close to extinction. For the Exmoor ponies you see these days we have to thank Sir Thomas Dyke Ackland, the landowner who leased Winsford Hill to the National Trust.

Today there are only about 1,000 ponies in the world. The 150 on Exmoor are in 11 herds, two of them in the care of the National Park Authority.

The waymarked path crosses stiles and footbridges, then passes through a gate into a short, hedged way. After a stile it follows the left edge of a long field, below **Waterhouse Farm**, to a double stile. Now bear slightly left to a stile with a hedged track going uphill beyond.

Walk 5

WHAT TO LOOK FOR ⓘ
The characteristic Exmoor field boundary is the **hedge bank** planted with beeches. Some of these may go back to the Iron Age or even earlier. They should be cut back and laid – the saplings are interwoven to make a formidable barrier. More often they have been left to grow out; the resulting profusion of beech leaves is particularly splendid in autumn.

This track will be our return route. At the track foot turn right to a stile. Cross a field next to a railed fence on the right, with a narrow strip of wild meadowsweet along the river bank beyond. At the corner cross a stone footbridge to a wooden one, and continue on the riverbank. Ignore two kissing gates on the left, but cross a stile ahead into an open field.

At the end of this field turn uphill at a signpost on a boggy path with a hedge on the right, to a gateway. Here another sign points towards **Brightworthy Farm**. Pass through gates immediately to the right of the buildings, into a fenced-off path around a field edge. A bridge on the left leads to steps down into a earth track. Turn right and, as the track fades out, pass a concrete shed to follow the bottom edges of two fields. The moorland is one field above, and the river now about two fields below. The trench of a little-used trackway descends gently to a gate leading on to the open moor.

You are most likely to see ponies at quiet times of the day. They live wild on the moors year-round. Evolution has given them a thick weatherproof coat, tough hooves, and a raised ridge around the eye (the so-called 'toad eye') to cast off rain, as well as enough speed and endurance to escape from the sabre-tooth tiger that once hunted them. But every Exmoor pony belongs to someone and every autumn they are gathered, inspected for disease and branded.

From here you could extend your walk to the medieval **Landacre Bridge**, visible ½ mile (800m) ahead – a suitable spot for your picnic (assuming you have remembered to put it in your rucksack). Otherwise turn left, following a sign for **Withypool Common**. A faint, rutted path follows the hedge that forms the upper boundary of the enclosed ground. The way slants uphill, then bends left and levels off.

The path gets clearer, and follows the hedge bank just below. It crosses a tarred driveway running down into the fields. Soon afterwards you encounter the steep-sided stream valley of **Knighton Combe**. The path slants down to the right, crosses the stream at a shallow ford, and disappears.

Head downstream for about 100yds (91m) between rowans, then slant up the combe side to rejoin the field-top hedge. The path is now clear, running towards the road that runs down into **Withypool**. About 220yds (201m) before the road turn down left to a gate in a corner of the hedge. A lane runs downhill to a stile. Cross this and the stile ahead to rejoin the outward route. Turn right to a double stile and continue downstream to **Withypool Bridge**.

WHILE YOU'RE THERE
A couple of miles (3.2km) upstream is **Landacre Bridge** – you could include it in your walk, or drive there afterwards. Its medieval stonework has proved strong enough for today's traffic. There are picnic spots alongside the River Barle.

Walk 6

Wimbleball Lake and Haddon Hill

Natural and artificial landscapes merge on this route through wooded valley, heathy hill and across the mighty Wimbleball Dam.

•DISTANCE•	6 miles (9.7km)
•MINIMUM TIME•	3hrs
•ASCENT / GRADIENT•	750ft (230m) ▲▲▲
•LEVEL OF DIFFICULTY•	林林 林林 林林
•PATHS•	Rough descent, long climb, easy track between, 1 stile
•LANDSCAPE•	Deeply wooded valley followed by airy, open heathland
•SUGGESTED MAP•	aqua3 OS Outdoor Leisure 9 Exmoor
•START / FINISH•	Grid reference: SS 969285
•DOG FRIENDLINESS•	Leads for short section past Haddon Hill Farm, no swimming (dogs or people)
•PARKING•	Frogwell Lodge car park, Haddon Hill
•PUBLIC TOILETS•	At car park

BACKGROUND TO THE WALK

You'll probably find it hard to imagine an outward force of 3.3 tons per square foot (36 tonnes per square metre) but that is the force exerted by the waters of Wimbleball Lake against the wall which contains them.

Wimbleball Dam
Some 200,000 tons of crushed stone from a quarry at Bampton was used to construct the dam in the mid-1970s. Sand from Cullompton was chosen to impart a pinkish colour and match the local bedrock. It's made of concrete, though the surface texture vaguely imitates massive stonework; and the 13 buttresses have no particular structural purpose but, aesthetically, they prevent it from looking too huge. The dam took four years to build, and the reservoir behind it needed another year just to fill up.

Water Cycled and Recycled
The reservoir holds almost 5 billion gallons (23 billion litres), which is enough to supply the whole South West peninsula for 44 days, or a town like Bridgwater for 9½ years. Its main job is to store water from the winter through into summer. It is also used to maintain the water level in the River Exe. When the river is full, a pipeline pumps water from Exebridge near Dulverton up into the reservoir. For the rest of the time the same pipeline, working the other way, delivers water to Dulverton. And, when it's really dry, the reservoir releases water into the Haddeo below the dam and so back into the Exe. Some of this will be water that had already flowed down the Exe during the previous winter.

A Multi-purpose Reservoir
Some 50 years ago water boards took the view that humans were dirty beasts who shouldn't be allowed anywhere near their own drinking water. However, Wimbleball was planned

from the start to provide not only drinking water but also recreation: fishing water, sailing water and walk-around-it water. (If you've half a day to spare, you can do a complete circuit on a waymarked path.) The woodland that looks so natural was planned by landscape architect Dame Sylvia Crowe and planted just 30 years ago, with the trees around the car park being the first to go in. Sadly, nothing can be done about the ugly and barren foreshore, since no plant can establish itself on ground that is submerged for months at a time. But, thanks to careful management, the weird, rattling cry of the nightjar now floats across the drinking water.

To finish with, here are some more numbers to ponder as you are walking: 1½ million people live downstream from Wimbleball Lake and drink its water, but every year 2 million sail on it, fish from it, or just walk down to its shores to have a look.

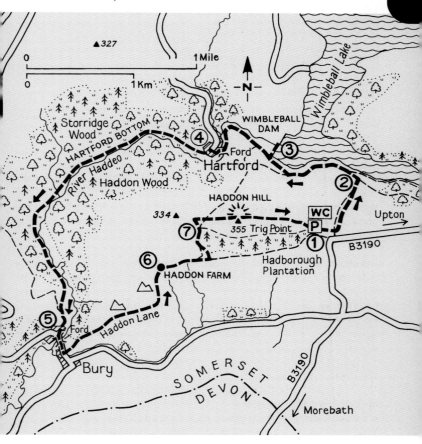

Walk 6 Directions

① Leave the car park by a small gate 50yds (46m) to the left of the toilet block. Turn right to cross a tarred track, then head straight downhill on a small path. This runs down through gorse, grass and heather until open birch woods give rise to easier going. If you lose the path just keep going downhill. Just above the reservoir you meet a stony track.

Walk 6

② Turn left on this. It emerges into open grassland and starts rising to the left. Watch out for a stile down on the right, into woodland. Across this, turn left on a small path that emerges near the **Wimbleball Dam**. A side-trip on to the dam gives fine views of Hartford Bottom below.

> **WHAT TO LOOK FOR** ⓘ
> Haddon Hill is the largest area of heathland in the Brendons. In June or July you may see the **heath fritillary**. This is a fairly small butterfly, coloured brown and reddish-orange; within the UK it flies only in a few scattered spots in the far south.

> **WHILE YOU'RE THERE** ⓘ
> **Dulverton**, the so-called capital of Exmoor, remains an attractive small town. It has a very good selection of cafés and pubs, and the Exmoor Information Centre in Fore Street is a useful entry point for the National Park.

③ Return along the dam and turn right into a descending tarmac lane signed 'Bury 2½'. At the bottom keep ahead on a concrete path signed 'Bridleway'. With a bridge ahead, bear left on to a grass track, this time signposted 'Bridleway to Bury'. It leads to a ford, so watch out for the footbridge on the right. Once across, take a track between houses, to turn left out into **Hartford**.

> **WHERE TO EAT AND DRINK** ⓘ
> **Lowtrow Cross Inn** is on the B3190, 2 miles (3.2km) east of Wheddon Hill car park. It's an old drover's halt, and in a sense carries on the trade, though travellers now park caravans, not cows, in the field alongside. There is a summer tea shop at Cowlings on the west side of the reservoir.

④ Turn left ('Bury 2') on a well-used track, partly tarred, partly mud. It passes through woods of oak and beech beside the **River Haddeo.** The track is now stony to the little village of **Bury**.

⑤ Turn left to the packhorse bridge beside the road's ford. Ignore a riverside track on the left and continue for 180yds (165m) to turn left at a bridleway sign. Here pass between houses to a sign for **Haddon Hill**, and a sunken track. This climbs steeply, with a stream in its bottom that flows over orange bedrock. At the top it continues as a green (or brown) track between grown-out hedges, before turning left for another short climb to **Haddon Farm**.

⑥ Pass to the left of the farm's buildings, on to its access track. After ¼ mile (400m) this reaches the corner of a wood. After another 70yds (64m) a stile above leads into the wood. Ignore the pointing signpost but bear left to go up the left-hand side of the wood to a gate on to the open hill. Go up alongside the wood to its top corner.

⑦ Take a track that bears left to cross the crest of the hill. Here turn sharp right, on a wide track that runs to the top of **Haddon Hill**. Continue downhill, through thin, peaty soil that grows only some sparse grasses, to the car park.

Hawk Combe and Porlock Hill

A stiff climb through the wildwood for a sudden sea view.

•DISTANCE•	6 miles (9.7km)
•MINIMUM TIME•	3hrs 15min
•ASCENT / GRADIENT•	1,200ft (370m) ▲▲▲
•LEVEL OF DIFFICULTY•	🚶🚶 🚶🚶 🚶
•PATHS•	Initial stiff climb then smooth, well-marked paths, no stiles
•LANDSCAPE•	Steep woodland, leading on to open heath
•SUGGESTED MAP•	aqua3 OS Outdoor Leisure 9 Exmoor
•START / FINISH•	Grid reference: SS 885468
•DOG FRIENDLINESS•	Deer and wild ponies so dogs must be under control
•PARKING•	Pay-and-display at Porlock Central Car Park; free parking at Whitstone Post, Point ⑤
•PUBLIC TOILETS•	At car park, and in Mill Lane

BACKGROUND TO THE WALK

A wood used to be something that just happened: a patch of ground too steep for the plough and too far from the village to be cut for firewood. Sometimes a patch of trees in a field corner turns out to have been there since the ancient wildwood covered the land at the end of the Ice Age. This is shown by the number and variety of its plant species, in particular its lichens; and by certain sorts of tree, such as the small-leaved lime. The Exmoor coast is rich in such woodland and in Hawk Combe the woods are amongst the oldest in Somerset.

Ancient Oaks

On the sandstone soils and under the warm rainfall of the Exmoor combes the natural cover is an oak wood, specifically sessile oak. The more familiar common oak has its acorns on stalks, while the sessile's ones grow straight on the twig; in addition, the sessile oak's leaves are longer and less rounded than those of the common oak.

Under the oaks grow native shrubs such as hazel and whitebeam. Our many sorts of native woodlice, leaf aphids and tree creepers flourish best on our native trees: they don't like nasty 'foreign' food like the horse chestnut. Dormice live in the hazel thickets, and the pied flycatcher darts through the green gloom. This bird prefers the western woods – some naturalists say that this is because the sessile oak, being lower and more spreading, gives better flight-paths; others think it's just because these woods are allowed more creative neglect: rotten branches drop off, leaving handy nest-holes.

Porlock Hill

If the climb through the woods of Hawk Combe is steep for feet, the A39 is equally so for wheels. It climbs 800ft in a mile (240m in 1.6km), with the steepest bit at the bottom. Extra horses were stationed at Porlock for attaching to the coaches here. Two-thirds of the way up stands a traditional AA phone box in yellow and black. This has been retained as a memory of the days when steam would jet from your radiator and the helpful AA man would come on his motorbike with a can of water. Modern cars can manage the ascent, though drivers who stall their engines may still have considerable trouble with a hill start on a 1 in 4 (25%) gradient. Coming down, though, there's still potential energy to be got rid of at roughly the rate of a one-bar electric fire. Those who neglect to engage low gear will end up with very hot brake discs – in Porlock car park you may catch the burnt-toast aroma of a car recently arrived from the west.

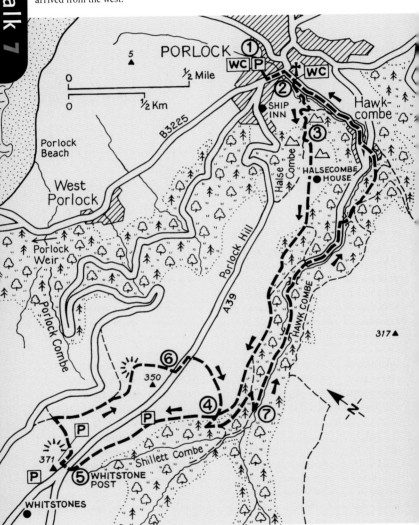

Walk 7 **Directions**

① From the car park follow signs for the public library and then turn left. Just before the church turn right into **Parsons Street**. At a small parking area with toilets a bridleway sign for Hawkcombe points upstream to a footbridge.

WHILE YOU'RE THERE
The best side-trip is actually another walk… From the tiny port of Porlock Weir it's 1 mile (1.6km) each way through the woods to **Culbone church**. It's the smallest in England: no road reaches it, and it's where Coleridge wrote *Kubla Khan*; church services are held every other Sunday.

② The path climbs through bamboo and laurel, to join another bridleway from below. It zig-zags steeply up through the wood, to pass below a wall with a small inset bench. At the top of this low wall the paths divide.

③ Turn left, still climbing, and at once bear right into a sunken path. Emerging at a white house, called **Halsecombe**, keep ahead to a field gate marked with a blue spot. Follow the left edge of a field, to the left-hand of two gates; it leads back into woodland. Take the bridleway ahead, with occasional blue waymarkers. The narrow track becomes a terraced path, running near the top edge of the wood for a mile (1.6km) to reach a track.

④ Turn left down the track for just a few paces, and then turn right into a path signed 'Whitstone Post': this is narrow, with gorse

WHERE TO EAT AND DRINK
Porlock has a wide selection of attractive pubs and cafés. The **Royal Oak** was the preferred pub of R D Blackmore. It was closed down because of rowdiness in 1880 but has since mended its ways; it is inexpensive and welcomes dogs. The **Ship** (at the foot of Porlock Hill) was frequented by Coleridge and his circle – and also by Blackmore's fictional highwayman, Tom Faggus.

encroaching; it then runs through bracken and heather with views into the head of Hawk Combe. As the path enters a thicket of hawthorns bear right to reach the road signpost at **Whitstone Post**.

⑤ Cross the main **A39** into a parking area, and turn right on a wide heather path. After 110yds (100m) turn left down a broad track. Where it turns left, turn right into a smaller track. This contours through gorse and heather, with superb views over Porlock Bay, then rejoins the A39 at a cattle grid.

⑥ Turn left, then right into a track signposted as a bridleway to **Porlock**. Cross two cattle grids to reach Point ④ of the upward route. Keep on down the track for another 125yds (114m), then turn left into a small, terraced path. This runs gently downhill for ¼ mile (400m), to meet a wider path. Turn sharp right down to the stream.

⑦ A broad path runs downstream. On reaching some houses it becomes a tarred lane and descends through a wood. At a high wall on the right a footpath sign points to a footbridge. Over this, the path ascends gently through the woods for 220yds (201m). Bear left on a path marked 'No Horses' and gently descend to join a street at a small parking area. Turn left to cross the stream, then turn right into **Mill Lane** and Porlock.

WHAT TO LOOK FOR
About 300yds (274m) uphill from Whitstone Post and 50yds (46m) to the left of the A39 are the **Whitstones** themselves. They were thrown there in a contest between a giant and the Devil.

Walk 8

Horner's Corners

On the trail of Exmoor's red deer in the woodlands under Dunkery Beacon.

•DISTANCE•	4½ miles (7.2km)
•MINIMUM TIME•	2hrs 30min
•ASCENT / GRADIENT•	1,000ft (300m) ▲▲▲
•LEVEL OF DIFFICULTY•	⅓⅓ ⅓⅓ ⅓⅓
•PATHS•	Broad paths, with some stonier ones, steep in places, no stiles
•LANDSCAPE•	Dense woodland in steep-sided stream valleys
•SUGGESTED MAP•	aqua3 OS Outdoor Leisure 9 Exmoor
•START / FINISH•	Grid reference: SS 898455
•DOG FRIENDLINESS•	Off lead, but be aware of deer and horse-riders
•PARKING•	National Trust car park (free) at Horner
•PUBLIC TOILETS•	At car park

BACKGROUND TO THE WALK

Horner takes its name from the Saxon 'hwrnwr', a wonderfully expressive word meaning snorer, that here describes the rumble of the stream in its enclosed valley. Above the treetops, Webber's Post is a splendid viewpoint out across the Bristol Channel. What Mr Webber stood there to view, though, was the hunting of red deer.

The herd on Exmoor numbers several thousand. Although this is small compared to those in the Scottish Highlands, the Exmoor stag himself is the UK's biggest wild deer. This is simply because his life is slightly easier – farmed deer are larger again. On Exmoor, as in the rest of Northern Europe outside Scotland, the deer remains a forest animal. Exmoor's mix of impenetrable woodland with areas of open grazing, even with all its houses, farms and fields, remains good deer country.

The calf is born dappled for camouflage under the trees, and lies in shelter during the day while the hind feeds. If you do come across a deer calf, leave it alone – it hasn't been abandoned. During the summer the stags and hinds run in separate herds. In the Scottish Highlands deer graze on high ground during the day to escape from midges, and descend to the forest at night; on Exmoor the main annoying pest is the human, so the deer graze the moor at dawn and dusk, and spend the day in the trees.

Stag Nights

In September and October comes the spectacular rut, when stags roar defiance at each other, and, if that fails, do battle with antlers for mating privileges. During this time they eat only occasionally, fight a lot and mate as often as possible. The stag with a mighty roar and a hard head can gather a harem of a dozen hinds. Your best chance of seeing one is very early or very late in the day – or else in the forest. I have had a bramble patch beside my path suddenly start bouncing around like an angry saucepan of milk, until, after ten seconds, a half-grown calf burst out of the middle of it and ran away. You may well smell the deer, even though it probably smelled you first and has already gone quietly away. Look closely, too, at the small brown cows two fields away – they may well be deer. I've seen grazing deer from a train window just five minutes out of Taunton Station, though they were the smaller roe.

While deer are thriving, it's the Exmoor stag hunters that are in danger of extinction. Just one pack of the traditional staghounds remains. Following pressure from its own members, the National Trust has banned hunting from its land, and the national government is set to ban it altogether when it finds the parliamentary time.

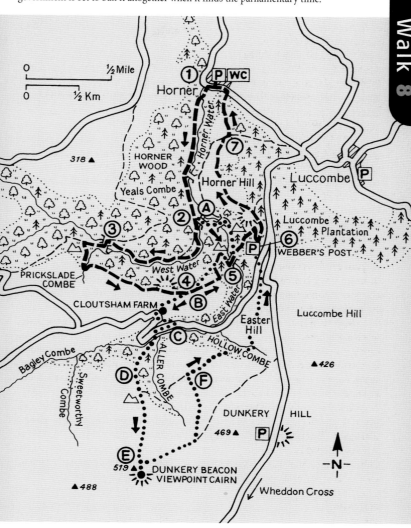

Walk 8 Directions

① Leave the National Trust car park in Horner village past the toilets and turn right to the track leading into **Horner Wood**. This crosses a bridge and passes a field

before rejoining **Horner Water**. You can take a footpath alongside the stream instead of the track, they lead to the same place. Ignore the first footbridge, and continue along the obvious track to where a sign, 'Dunkery Beacon', points off to the left towards a second footbridge.

② Ignore this footbridge as well (unless you're on Walk 9). Keep on the track for another 100yds (91m), then fork left on a path alongside **West Water**. This rejoins the track, and after another ½ mile (800m) a bridleway sign points back to the right. Here look down to the left for a footbridge. For me this was a thrilling balancing act on two girders – but the rebuilding of the bridge (swept away in floods in 2001) has now been completed.

③ Cross on to a path that slants up to the right. After 200yds (183m) turn left into a smaller path that turns uphill alongside **Prickslade Combe**. The path reaches the combe's little stream at a cross-path, with the wood top visible above. Here turn left, across the stream, on a path contouring through the top of the wood. It emerges into the open and arrives at a tree with a bench and a fine view over the top of the woodlands to **Porlock Bay**.

④ Continue ahead on a grassy track, with the car park of **Webber's Post** clearly visible ahead. Alas, the deep valley of the **East Water** lies

---

WHERE TO EAT AND DRINK ⓘ
Delightful Horner village has not one but two excellent **tea shops**, each with an outdoor seating area and ice creams. Those who would prefer beer or, of course, a glass of cider should head for the fleshpots of Porlock (▶ Walk 7).

between you and your destination. So, turn down left on a clear path back into birchwoods. This zig-zags down to meet a larger track in the valley bottom.

⑤ Turn downstream, crossing a footbridge over the **East Water**, beside a ford. After about 60yds (55m) bear right on to an ascending path. At the top of the steep section turn right on a small sunken path that climbs gently to **Webber's Post** car park.

⑥ Walk to the left, round the car park, to a path marked 'Permitted Bridleway' to **Horner**. (Do not take the pink-surfaced, easy-access path immediately to the right.) After 80yds (73m) bear left on to a wider footpath. Keep ahead down a wide, gentle spur, with the deep valley of the **Horner Water** on your left. As the spur steepens, the footpath meets a crossing track signposted '**Windsor Path**'.

⑦ Turn right for perhaps 30 paces, then take a descending path signposted '**Horner**'. Narrow at first, this widens and finally meets a wide, horse-mangled track with wooden steps; turn left down this into **Horner**.

WHILE YOU'RE THERE ⓘ
Dunster Castle has everything – battlements and gardens, a wooded hill setting with an ancient village below, a working water mill, the national collection of strawberry trees (*Arbutus unedo*) and even a somewhat implausible King Arthur legend – he helped St Carantoc tame the local dragon.

WHAT TO LOOK FOR ⓘ
Multiple tree trunks growing from a single point show where the woodland has formerly been **coppiced**. Every ten years the new shoots would be cut back to the original stump. This method of harvesting a woodland is more productive than clear-felling and replanting, whether what you're after is oak bark for the tanning industry or just firewood. Coppicing has also allowed the original woodland plants to survive through the centuries.

Fire at Dunkery Beacon

A moorland extension leads up to the high point of Somerset.
See map and information panel for Walk 8

•DISTANCE•	6 miles (9.7km)
•MINIMUM TIME•	3hrs 40min
•ASCENT / GRADIENT•	1,700ft (520m) ▲▲▲
•LEVEL OF DIFFICULTY•	🚶🚶 🚶🚶 🚶🚶
•PATHS•	Rough paths in Horner Woods, stony hill descent, 2 stiles

Walk 9 Directions (Walk 8 option)

At Point ② of Walk 8, Point Ⓐ, turn left over the bridge, signposted 'Dunkery Beacon'. A wide path leads up **East Water**, crossing to its left side by ford and footbridge. After ¼ mile (400m) it crosses back, and very shortly a path branches off on the right. It climbs in zig-zags, and then more gently, to a cross-track and bench, Point Ⓑ, (also Point ④ on Walk 8). Cross the path and ascend to a gate. Follow the left edge of a field to another gate and stile, to a track to **Cloutsham Farm**. Turn left past the buildings, and, where the road bends, descend a track to rejoin the road lower down, Point Ⓒ.

Turn up the road, past a picnic field. Just after a bridge on the left a stream runs down to join the **East Water** and, a few steps further on, a wide path sets off across the stream, up the wooded spur and on to the open hill, Point Ⓓ.

After 120yds (110m) a contouring path crosses your own: this is **Dicky's Path**. To bypass Dunkery Hill simply turn left here to pass through the woods of **Aller Combe** and continue from Point Ⓕ; otherwise follow the clear path uphill. As the slope eases a wider, stony path joins from the left – this will be your descent route. The huge cairn is just beyond, Point Ⓔ.

Near by is a viewpoint cairn, with a topograph. Follow the ascent route back for 110yds (100m) and bear right on the wider, stony path. This runs down to the tip of **Aller Combe**, now a mere groove in the heather. After another 25yds (23m) turn down left on a smaller path. After 600yds (549m) it passes three hawthorns and shortly a fourth one marks the junction with Dicky's Path, Point Ⓕ.

Turn right on **Dicky's Path**, contouring through heather and thorn. It runs in and out of the steeply wooded **Hollow Combe**, where the path is protected with a handrail. Walk softly, for here you might see red deer.(Some say that if you smile and wave the deer will consider you a harmless idiot and allow you to approach more closely, but it's never worked for me.) When you emerge on to open ground fork left on a smaller path, through gorse and heather, to **Webber's Post** car park, Point ⑥.

Walk 10

Above the Severn Sea

From Porlock to Minehead along paths well-trodden by smugglers, coastguards and a famous poet.

•DISTANCE•	7¾ miles (12.5km)
•MINIMUM TIME•	4hrs
•ASCENT / GRADIENT•	1,050ft (320m) ▲▲▲
•LEVEL OF DIFFICULTY•	🚶 🚶 🚶
•PATHS•	Coast path, one steep, exposed, avoidable section, 1 stile
•LANDSCAPE•	Moorland, grassland and wood, high above sea
•SUGGESTED MAP•	aqua3 OS Outdoor Leisure 9 Exmoor
•START•	Grid reference: SS 886467
•FINISH•	Grid reference: SS 972468
•DOG FRIENDLINESS•	Open land, dogs must be under control
•PARKING•	Pay-and-display all along Minehead seafront
•PUBLIC TOILETS•	Porlock, Bossington, Minehead Harbour
•NOTE•	Buses 37 and 300 run year-round, frequent service in summer; timetables from tourist information centre

Walk 10 Directions

From **Porlock church** take the street signposted 'Museum' and turn left into **Sparkhayes Lane** until steps on the right lead into **Bay Road**. At its end, turn left into a hedged path. This leads through kissing gates into a hedged track. Turn right on a lane into the thatched village of **Bossington**.

Pass to the right of the car park to a footbridge. A track on the left runs by the river, then climbs on to open hill. After 300yds (274m) it passes a National Trust collecting cairn. Here note the path on the right climbing into **Hurlstone Combe**, before continuing ahead to the old coastguard viewpoint on **Hurlstone Point**.

During the 18th century, as a measure against smuggling, coastguards walked the coastal path, all night and in all weathers, one man for every quarter-mile (400m). Almost every officer and man in the Royal Navy must have taken part either in smuggling or in its prevention. The resulting skill in foul weather seamanship and coastal raiding certainly contributed to the Navy's success against Napoleon Bonaparte.

The path ahead traverses a steep, exciting and atmospheric corner of the coastline. It should be avoided when slippery (after heavy rain) and in high winds: you may prefer to avoid it altogether. The alternative is to retrace your steps

> **WHERE TO EAT AND DRINK** ⓘ
> Beautifully placed at the corner of Minehead Harbour, the **Old Ship Aground** is pet-friendly and decorated with bits of real ships. The nearby **Mother Leaky's Parlour** café invites dogs to claim a free sausage, and also welcomes well-behaved owners.

along the arrival path then fork left on to a slightly higher one. Above the NT cairn, turn on to the path up **Hurlstone Combe**. Adventurous souls will continue from the lookout over a stile. The narrow path contours around the headland into a shallow combe formed by landslips. Look out for a path turning sharply back to the right, to zig-zag up the combe side. The spur above is rocky, so the path continues just down to the right of the crest, to the signpost at the head of Hurlstone Combe. Turn uphill on a broad path, soon with the cairn of **Selworthy Beacon** ahead. In the dip before this, note where the coast path forks off to the left, but keep ahead to the top of Selworthy Beacon.

Return down the path for 80yds (73m) then fork right to rejoin the coast path. Follow its clear track just above enclosed pastures. Far out to sea you'll see the buildings of **Bridgend** in Wales. In the north east are the islands of Flat Holm and Steep Holm. Flat Holm is in Wales, Steep Holm in England: their names reflect their profiles.

The Exmoor coast path was a favourite of the poet Samual Taylor Coleridge while he was living at Nether Stowey (▶ Walk 13). Three times he completed the 45 miles (72km) from the Quantocks to Lynton in a single day.

As you pass above **Grexy Combe**, fork left on a sunken way between gorse bushes. This rises to a gate. Follow a coast path sign to keep on the same level for another ½ mile (800m), to a bench and signpost with a car park just above. Here turn steeply downhill, signposted 'Sea Front via Coastpath'. After

WHAT TO LOOK FOR ⓘ

South West Coast Path walkers: those with the sea on their left will be on the last steps of their long walk. They'll be recognisable by their large rucksacks and weatherworn appearance. Those coming the other way will have sparkling equipment, and an eager air. Fewer than half of them will actually reach Poole Harbour…

200yds (183m) a more pleasant path turns off to the right. This becomes a splendid, broad and gentle terrace path, through a steep oakwood. It eventually becomes a track, reaching tarmac on the edge of Minehead. The next bend brings a view ahead of the tent-like **Butlin's Holiday Camp**.

The South West Coast Path, at 600-odd miles (970km), is Britain's longest National Trail. This was achieved by re-establishing the coastguard path as a continuous right of way, a process which took the best part of 30 years. The result is a surprisingly steep and windy walk. The route is thoroughly waymarked, as 'Coastpath' (oddly, signposted as a single word on the Somerset section).

At a road junction turn sharp left into a tarred path that descends in zig-zags. Turn left down tarmac steps to the **Quayside**. Ahead, a pair of aluminium map-reading arms are the marker for the end or beginning of the rather longer coast path right round to Dorset.

WHILE YOU'RE THERE ⓘ

Exmoor Falconry and Animal Farm is just off the walk at Bossington. It has cuddly rabbits, friendly ferrets and the chance to have an owl alight on your outstretched fist. It also offers full-day falconry outings on Exmoor.

From Wheddon Cross to Brendon's Heights

A sunken lane from Wheddon Cross leads up to Lype Hill, the high point of the Brendons.

•DISTANCE•	5¾ miles (9.2km)
•MINIMUM TIME•	3hrs
•ASCENT / GRADIENT•	850ft (260m) ▲▲▲
•LEVEL OF DIFFICULTY•	👥 👥 👥
•PATHS•	A rugged track, then little-used field bridleways, 4 stiles
•LANDSCAPE•	Rounded hills with steep, wooded sides
•SUGGESTED MAP•	aqua3 OS Outdoor Leisure 9 Exmoor
•START / FINISH•	Grid reference: SS 923387
•DOG FRIENDLINESS•	Mostly pasture, where dogs must be closely managed
•PARKING•	Village car park (free) on A396 at Wheddon Cross
•PUBLIC TOILETS•	At car park

BACKGROUND TO THE WALK

This walk takes in the highest point of the Brendons, Lype Hill, at 1,390ft (423m). The wrap-around view includes Dunkery Beacon, Wales and Dartmoor. The trig point itself stands on an ancient tumulus; the second apparent tumulus near by houses a modern-day water tank.

Brown Hill

Brendon means 'brown hill'. The shales and muddy sandstones are sea-bottom rocks: though the oldest in Somerset, they formed from the decomposition of still older mountains that have now completely disappeared. The Brendons are not particularly high, and are farmed to their tops, though the steeper sides are wooded. The scene appears timeless, but is actually rather recent: the hilltops were forested into the Middle Ages, and later became an industrial estate.

Return of the Iron Age

The Iron Age on Brendon saw the digging of long ramparts across the plateau, and a great settlement on the high ground. However, apart from a small fort at Elworthy Barrows, this activity wasn't in pre-Roman times, but in the more recent 19th century. A railway ran along the Brendon ridge from the iron ore mines. At its eastern end was a form of engineering we no longer see, except in Switzerland: a rope-assisted incline taking ore down to valley level. The ore then passed along the mineral railway to Watchet and the smelters of South Wales.

Below the mining areas and the farmland the hillsides have been less disturbed by man. Here, altitude, thin soils, and western levels of rainfall mean a sort of woodland more akin to the Scottish Highlands. You'll see the silver birch, for example – silver and gold if you're lucky enough to be here in late October. As well as a variety of autumn fungi in vivid colours, Hartcleeve has striking examples of Witch's Broom in its birch trees. These twig-clusters resemble untidy spherical nests but are in fact caused by a fungus infection (*ascomycete*) which interferes with the tree's growth hormones. A really well-established Witch's Broom can be 3ft (1m) across and will consist of hundreds of twigs.

The Sinking of Lanes

Putham Lane shows several centuries' worth of erosion in action: a speeded-up version of what's happening to the hills as a whole over millions of years (rather than a few hundred). Looking through the hedge you can see how much lower the lane is than the surrounding fields. Where the lane steepens, it also gets more deeply dug in; at its steepest point you can see bare grey bedrock in its floor. Where the track has dug itself down below the water table, a permanent stream trickles down it. After rain or during snowmelt this stream becomes a flood. Even at its low summer level, it's easy to see how it combines with feet (and, latterly, wheels) to excavate the track.

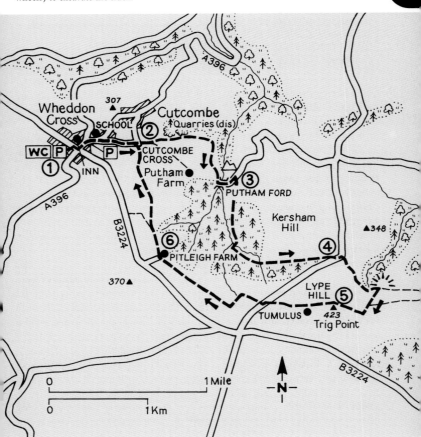

Walk 11 Directions

① From the main crossroads head towards Dunster, and bear right at the war memorial to pass a small car park on the right-hand side. After the school, bear right, following the signpost to **Puriton**. This is **Popery Lane** – and yes, the school we just passed was a Roman Catholic one. The sunken lane runs

Walk 11

to **Cutcombe Cross**, where you keep ahead ('Luxburough via Putham Ford') then bear left at a sign into **Putham Lane**.

② Horses and tractors also use this narrow hedged track. At the bottom it crosses a ford, with a stone footbridge alongside. Now keep ahead on to a climbing lane surfaced with eroded tarmac.

> ### WHILE YOU'RE THERE
> Bluebell woods are fairly common around Exmoor. However, a wood carpeted in snowdrops is more unusual. **Snowdrop Wood** at Wheddon Cross has caused traffic jams in the past and Exmoor National Park Authority now runs a park-and-ride scheme: this departs from the village car park during the February snowdrop season.

> ### WHERE TO EAT AND DRINK ⓘ
> The **Rest And Be Thankful Inn** is beside the car park, and offers bar meals and real ales. Dogs can be accommodated in the downstairs dining area.

③ At the top of the steep climb a field gate on the right has an inconspicuous footpath signpost. It leads on to a green track that runs below and then into a wood. Watch out for a footpath sign and a stile beside a stream below. Cross the water and take a small path on its right, into an open space. A slightly wider path above slants up along a bracken clearing. After a stile it follows the foot of a wood, to join a forest road and then a tarred lane.

④ Turn left, down a wide verge, and take the upper of two gates on the right: the correct one has a stile and footpath sign. Head up the side of a wooded combe and across its top. Now a sea view is on the left, a stile and gate ahead. Don't cross,

but turn right, and right again across the top of the field to a gate beside the trig point on **Lype Hill**.

⑤ Through the gate keep ahead across a field, with a tumulus 70yds (64m) away on the left, and after a gate bear left to follow the fence on the left to its corner. A gate ahead leads on to a road. Cross to a signposted gate, and bear left to the field's far corner. Turn left alongside a beech bank to a waymarked gate. Here turn right, with a fence on your right, and head down along field edges towards **Pitleigh Farm**. An awkward gate in deer fencing leads on to the driveway just to the left of the farm.

⑥ Cross the driveway into a green track. This becomes a fenced-in field edge to a deer-fence gate on the left. Turn right to continue as before with hedges now on your right. After two fields you reach a hedged track. This runs down to the crossroads in **Popery Lane**.

> ### WHAT TO LOOK FOR ⓘ
> Red, yellow and blue! In England the various **rights of way** are colour-coded. Through Highley Plantation you're on a footpath: look out for yellow paint-spots and waymarkers. Every gate after Lype Hill has the blue mark of a bridleway. Here there will be no stiles, but only gates, as horses can't climb stiles. At the start of the route, on Puriton Lane, a red mark shows the way through the wood. Here you are on a byway, in theory open to all traffic – although you are unlikely to meet a Rolls Royce coming the other way.

Walk 12

Quantock Coastline: Kilve and East Quantoxhead

With the risk of French invasion now passed, you can spy out these Tudor villages and breezy cliffs without fearing arrest.

•DISTANCE•	3 miles (4.8km)
•MINIMUM TIME•	1hr 30min
•ASCENT / GRADIENT•	250ft (80m)
•LEVEL OF DIFFICULTY•	
•PATHS•	Tracks, field paths, and grassy cliff top, 7 stiles
•LANDSCAPE•	Tudor villages, farmland and coastline
•SUGGESTED MAP•	aqua3 OS Explorer 140 Quantock Hills & Bridgwater
•START / FINISH•	Grid reference: ST 144442
•DOG FRIENDLINESS•	Extra care along cliff top, unstable near edge
•PARKING•	Pay-and-display at sea end of Sea Lane
•PUBLIC TOILETS•	At car park (closed October – February)

BACKGROUND TO THE WALK

With two Tudor villages, industrial remnants up to only a century ago, and a lucid display of geology underfoot, this is a walk to stimulate the brain as well as the lungs.

Jobs for the Priests

The chantry chapel at Kilve is built in the local grey shale, but with the arches picked out in orange Quantock sandstone. The sandstone is easier to work into shaped blocks, but has been eroded by the sea winds. This chantry housed five priests whose sole function was the saying of prayers and masses for the deceased Simon de Furneaux and his family. The doctrine was that the rich could pay their way out of purgatory by setting up such chapels. This created employment for priests, but contributed to the general loss of credibility of the Catholic faith. In fact Kilve Chantry closed even before the Reformation, when a Lollard dissenter married into the family in the late-14th century. Later it was used by smugglers for storing brandy and burnt down around 1850 in an alcohol fire. Behind the ruins, the Chantry House has a pigeon loft still in use.

The old (possibly Saxon) preaching cross in Quantoxhead churchyard is a viewpoint for the Manor House. It also looks on to the back of Quantoxhead Farm, where the semi-circular wing is a horse-gang. This once housed a capstan where horses walked in circles to power, via an endless belt, farm machinery in the main building. The church itself has fossils incorporated into the walls, and Tudor-carved pew ends.

The Spies who Wrote Sonnets

When Samual Taylor Coleridge and William Wordsworth walked here, their particular interest was in the Holford stream. Coleridge planned a poem in his deceptively simple 'conversational' style, tracing the stream from its birth high in Hodder Combe (▶ Walk 13). However, the two poets had already aroused local suspicions by their comings and goings, and both had been enthusiastic supporters of the French Revolution in its early days. This was 1797: England was in the grip of invasion fever; and Kilve has a small but usable harbour. Accordingly, a government agent called James Walsh was sent to investigate. He quizzed a footman about their dinner-time conversation: it was reported as being quite impossible to understand, which was, of course, most suspicious. The agent followed them to Kilve. Lurking behind a gorse bush, he heard them discussing 'Spy Nosy' and thought he'd been found out. They had actually been talking about the German philosopher, Spinoza... Coleridge never got round to writing his poem *The Brook* – but Wordsworth did. Twenty years later, he adopted his friend's plan into a sequence of sonnets on Lakeland's River Duddon.

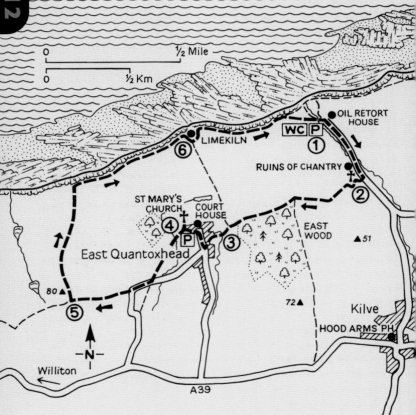

Walk 12 Directions

① From the car park head back along the lane to the ruined chantry. Turn into the churchyard through a lychgate. Such gates were built to shelter coffins and their bearers: this one is too small for its purpose, so must be a modern reconstruction. Pass to the left of the church, to a kissing gate.

② A signposted track crosses a field to a gate with a stile; bear right to another gate with a stile and pass along the foot of **East Wood**. (At its far end, a stile allows wandering

Walk 12

WHILE YOU'RE THERE ⓘ
The magnificent **Cleeve Abbey** at Washford is relatively little-known as it's only recently been made safe for visitors, under the care of English Heritage. The vaulted stone roof of the chapter house and the carved wooden one of the refectory are particularly impressive.

WHERE TO EAT AND DRINK ⓘ
Just ¼ mile (400m) into the walk are the tempting **Chantry Tea Gardens**. The nearest alcohol available is at the **Hood Arms**, a 17th-century coaching inn at Kilve – it welcomes walkers but not their muddy boots.

into the wood, from April to August only.) Ignoring the stile on the left, keep ahead to a field gate with a stile and a track crossing a stream.

③ The track bends left past gardens and ponds of **East Quantoxhead** to reach a tarred lane. Turn right, towards the Tudor **Court House**, but before its gateway bear left into a car park. Pass through to a tarred path beyond two kissing gates. In an open field this bears right, to **St Mary's Church**.

④ Return to the first kissing gate but don't go through, instead bearing right to a field gate, and crossing the field beyond to a lane. Turn right and, where the lane bends left, keep ahead into a green track. At its top, turn right at a 'Permissive path' noticeboard.

⑤ Follow field edges down to the cliff top, and turn right. A clifftop path leads to a stile before a sharp

dip, with a ruined limekiln opposite. This was built around 1770 to process limestone shipped from Wales into lime for the fields and for mortar. Most of the rest of Somerset is limestone, but it was still easier to bring it by sea across the Bristol Channel.

⑥ Turn around the head of the dip, and back left to the cliff top. Here an iron ladder descends to the foreshore: you can see alternating layers of blue-grey lias (a type of limestone) and grey shale. Fossils can be found here, but be aware that the cliffs are unstable – hard hats are now standard wear for geologists. Alternatively, given a suitably trained dog and the right sort of spear, you could pursue the traditional sport of 'glatting' – hunting conger eels in the rock pools. Continue along the wide clifftop path until a tarred path bears off to the right, crossing the stream studied by Coleridge, into the car park.

WHAT TO LOOK FOR ⓘ
On the approach to East Quantoxhead church look out for a fine **ammonite**, 12 inches (30cm) across, built into the wall on the right; it's 25yds (23m) before the kissing gate, and marked by a splash of yellow lichen. At the very end of the walk, as you come into the car park, on the left is the brick chimney of a short-lived **Oil Retort House** (for oil distillation) from 1924; there is oil in the grey shale, but it's less trouble to get it from Texas.

Walk 13

A Quantock Amble

An up-and-down walk in the Quantock combes.

•DISTANCE•	5½ miles (8.8km)
•MINIMUM TIME•	2hrs 40min
•ASCENT / GRADIENT•	700ft (210m) ▲▲▲
•LEVEL OF DIFFICULTY•	林林 林林 林林
•PATHS•	Wide, smooth paths, with one slightly rough descent, no stiles
•LANDSCAPE•	Deep, wooded hollows and rolling hilltops
•SUGGESTED MAP•	aqua3 OS Explorer 140 Quantock Hills & Bridgwater
•START / FINISH•	Grid reference: ST 154410
•DOG FRIENDLINESS•	Well-trained dogs can usually remain off leads throughout
•PARKING•	At back of Holford (free)
•PUBLIC TOILETS•	None on route

BACKGROUND TO THE WALK

The great beauty of these hills, says Dorothy Wordsworth, is their wild simplicity. We often hear of the 'Lakes poets', but in fact Coleridge wrote most of his best-known works (*Kubla Khan*, *Christabel*) while he was living in Somerset, and his neighbour, Wordsworth, started his poetic career here as well. Coleridge was the first to move to the Quantocks, invited by a friendly bookseller, from Nether Stowey, who had noticed a cottage to let at the bottom of his garden. A year later Wordsworth and his sister moved into the rather grand house of Alfoxton (now a hotel and passed towards the end of this walk).

This took place in the heady years after the French Revolution, and the ultimate aim of the two friends was to set up a sort of poets' commune, gathering like-minded radicals for a group emigration to America. In the meantime, the two young men revolutionised English poetry. They were key players in the Romantic Revival, overthrowing the stilted formal verse of the previous hundred years, by creating Romantic poetry as a means of describing and expressing strong emotion.

Amazingly, Coleridge's most celebrated work, *The Rime of the Ancient Mariner*, was written in the Quantocks at a time when his entire experience of sea voyaging was a crossing of the Severn by the Chepstow ferry. The poem was roughed out in the course of a walk taken by Coleridge, Wordsworth and Wordsworth's sister, Dorothy. They set out from Alfoxton at 4PM on a November afternoon in 1797; this was timed so that they could watch from the Quantock ridge as dusk gave way to moonlight over the Bristol Channel. After crossing the Quantocks they continued by the coast path (► Walk 10), finally arriving at Dulverton four days later. Coleridge's mesmeric *Christabel* recalls the wooded combes of Holford. In *This Lime-tree Bower My Prison*, Coleridge himself was frustratingly trapped at home in Stowey, after his wife Sara had spilt scalding milk on his foot.

> *'Now, my friends emerge*
> *Beneath the wide wide Heaven – and view again*
> *The many-steepled tract magnificent*
> *Of hilly fields and meadows, and the sea'*

Meanwhile, his friends were following your present walk up to Bicknoller Post and enjoying the view over the Bristol Channel. The different writing styles of the two friends were reflected in their walking styles: Coleridge liked to compose his verse whilst striding over awkward ground, whereas Wordsworth did so pacing up and down a gravel path.

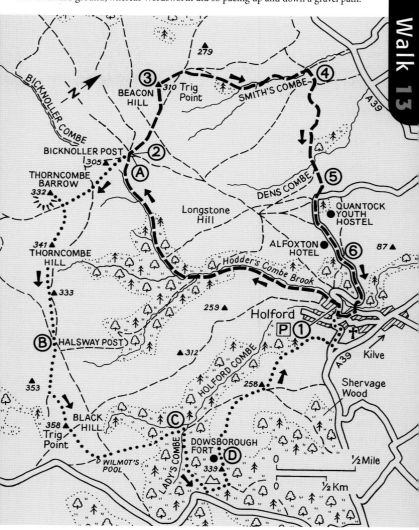

Walk 13 **Directions**

① Two tracks leave the road beside the car park. Take the right-hand one, which is marked with a bridleway sign. It becomes an earth track through woods, with

Hodder's Combe Brook on its right. After ¾ mile (1.2km) the small track fords the stream and forks. Take the right-hand option, entering a side-valley. The path runs up the valley floor, gradually rising through oakwoods floored with bilberry (locally known as 'whortleberry'), then mixed heather and bracken, to reach the **Quantock ridge**. As the ground eases, keep ahead over two cross-tracks to **Bicknoller Post**.

② To the right (north) of this col the ridge divides: we shall take the left-hand branch, which is '**Beacon Hill**', so pass to the left side of the marker stake on a broad track. Keep ahead on the widest of the tracks. This track becomes a double one, almost a 'dual carriageway'. Bear left off it to the trig point on **Beacon Hill**.

③ At the trig point bend half-right to another marker-post on the main track. A smaller path goes down directly ahead, into **Smith's Combe**. The path weaves around, crossing the stream several times.

> **WHERE TO EAT AND DRINK** ⓘ
> There is nothing currently at Holford. Nether Stowey has a good selection, with the **Royal Oak** being congenial and dog-friendly.

④ At the foot of the valley, with green fields below, is a 4-way 'Quantock Greenway' signpost: turn right (green arrow), uphill at first. The path runs around the base of the hills, with a belt of trees below and then the green fields. At the first spur crest is another signpost, 3-way: keep ahead for **Holford**. The path drops to cross a stream, **Dens**

> **WHILE YOU'RE THERE** ⓘ
> The **Coleridge Cottage** at Nether Stowey is managed by the National Trust. The lime tree bower is gone but you can see a bay tree planted by the poet, his massive inkwell, his sword and a lock of his hair as well as the rooms where he worked. The poet's privy has also survived. The cottage is open four afternoons a week except in winter.

Combe. After ¼ mile (400m) it drops towards a wide gate leading out on to tarmac.

⑤ Don't go through the gate, but strike uphill to another 'Quantock Greenway' signpost. Keep uphill (green arrow) to pass above a pink house on to a tarred lane. Take the patchily tarred track ahead below a couple of houses. A sign indicates the Quantock Hills Youth Hostel down to the left, but stay on the lane. It runs out past **Alfoxton**, with the walled garden of the grand house (once Wordsworth's, now a hotel) on the left and the stable block with its clock on the right. At the foot of the hotel driveway is a small parking area.

⑥ Follow the lane for 650yds (594m) then, as it bends right, look out for a waymarker and railings a little way down in the trees. Below is a spectacular footbridge leading across into **Holford**. Turn right, and at the first junction turn right again, to the car park.

> **WHAT TO LOOK FOR** ⓘ
> Just below Dowsborough Fort is, apparently, the home of the **Great Vurm** of Shervage Wood. It lives on sheep, cattle, whortleberries and people. It sometimes looks like a fallen tree trunk; the only person to have survived meeting it was a woodman from Stogumber who actually sat down on it to enjoy his lunchtime cider and sandwiches.
> A small building in the wood near the car park (grid ref ST 153411) is a **dog pound**. In the 18th century the huntsman at Alfoxton's kennels was killed by his own hounds when trying to pacify them from barking at stray dogs. Accordingly Alfoxton donated this pound to the community.

A Quantock Canter

Stretch your legs a little more along the extensive Quantock ridge.
See map and information panel for Walk 13

•DISTANCE•	8¾ miles (14.1km)
•MINIMUM TIME•	4hrs 30min
•ASCENT / GRADIENT•	1,500ft (450m) ▲▲▲
•LEVEL OF DIFFICULTY•	🚶🚶 🚶🚶 🚶🚶

Walk 14 Directions
(Walk 13 option)

'There are some heights in Wessex,
    shaped as if by a kindly hand
For thinking, dreaming, dying on;
    and at crises when I stand
Say on Ingpen Beacon eastward or on
    Wylls-Neck westwardly
I seem where I was before my birth,
    and after death shall be'

Thus wrote Thomas Hardy in
Wessex Heights (1896), making a
rare expedition out of his native
Dorset. Quantock's long, high-level
ridge is an invitation to a longer
and more vigorous walk – even if
you won't be able to keep up with
the horse-riders who find this open
heathland ideal for a breezy canter.

From **Bicknoller Post**, Point Ⓐ
(Point ② on Walk 13), keep ahead
for 25yds (23m), and turn left on
the main track. It skirts to the left of
a slight rise, to reach, after ¼ mile
(400m), the head of **Bicknoller
Combe**. At the top of the next rise
you can take a diversion to the right
to **Thorncombe Barrow**; its small
grassy hump is a fine viewpoint
away from the track traffic. Return
to the main track and follow it over
Thorncombe Hill to the col at
Halsway Post, Point Ⓑ.

Follow a fence up the next rise, and
turn left past tumuli to the trig
point on **Black Hill**. Bear left and
cross a track on to a wide, green
path. This descends gently to reach
a small pond, **Wilmot's Pool**. Here,
bear left on a rather muddy path.
After 200yds (183m) this goes
straight across a much wider track.
It descends gently into trees, and
then more steeply to the stream in
Lady's Combe, Point Ⓒ.

Cross and turn right, upstream. The
path follows the stream for 150yds
(137m) then slants uphill,
becoming rather steep at the top.
Where it reaches a cross path turn
left, up on to **Dowsborough Fort**.
Some stonework is visible as you
enter the fortifications. The path
keeps ahead just inside the earth
wall, in wet peaty ground, then
turns right to leave the rampart,
Point Ⓓ.

Head straight down the ridge on
the wide path, climb slightly to a
rise with a cairn, and continue
towards Holford, now visible below.
The path drops into woodland and
reaches a lane with the main A39
close by on the right. Turn left
towards Holford. Ignore the first
turnoff left, for **Holford Combe**,
and take the second, signposted
'YHA', to the car park.

Walk 15

River Parrett and Canal

From Bridgwater walk out beside a river and back beside a canal.

•DISTANCE•	5¼ miles (8.4km)
•MINIMUM TIME•	2hrs
•ASCENT / GRADIENT•	Negligible
•LEVEL OF DIFFICULTY•	
•PATHS•	Broad, made-up paths and a smaller riverside path, 3 stiles
•LANDSCAPE•	Reed beds and tidal riverside, tree-lined tow path
•SUGGESTED MAP•	aqua3 OS Explorer 140 Quantock Hills & Bridgwater
•START / FINISH•	Grid reference: ST 300370
•DOG FRIENDLINESS•	Off-lead on tow path and most of riverside; no fouling
•PARKING•	Pay-and-display in Dampier Street, near Blake Museum
•PUBLIC TOILETS•	At library in Dampier Street, close to car park

Walk 15 Directions

Turn right out of the car park, passing the end of **Blake Street** with its museum, to the Rose & Crown. Here, turn left into **St Mary's Street**, but at once bear left into **Old Taunton Road**. At its end a dual carriageway bridge crosses the **River Parrett**. Turn right, into a riverside lane signed 'Colley Lane Industrial Estate'. After 350yds (320m), opposite a fire station, concrete steps lead up and over the flood barrier to a gravel path. Follow this along the riverside for ¾ mile (1.2km) to a railway bridge, the **Somerset Bridge**; this has a footbridge attached. Once across, turn left under a low arch, well-scratched by motor traffic. Continue upstream on a lane with the River Parrett now on your left. Reed beds and flooded ground are on the right: these are the excavations of the former Bridgwater Brick and Tile Works. The use of this brick and tile for all of the older buildings gives the town its orangy-brown colouring.

The track turns aside to the right, but continue ahead next to the river and under the motorway. After one open field, a stile leads into the **Screech Owl Nature Reserve**. The reed beds were once the haunt of the bittern, a bird rather like a small brown heron, that hides in the reeds by pointing its neck and beak vertically upwards, and that has a strange booming cry – but it has not yet returned to Bridgwater. However, you may well see the sudden blue flash of a passing kingfisher, and the sharp-eyed may spot otter slides running down the mud into the river. I'm told that during the night the otters commute through the town centre

---

WHILE YOU'RE THERE

The **Blake Museum** at the start of the walk, is housed in a delightful botched-together cottage dating from various centuries. Bridgwater was originally a seaport, the largest in the county, and the museum commemorates one of Somerset's famous admirals – Robert Blake commander of Oliver Cromwell's navy. There is also a display on the Battle of Sedgemoor (► Walk 20).

to another flooded brickworks at Chilton Trinity. In June and July bird experts will be listening out for the very rare Cetti's warbler.

The path leaves the reserve at a second stile, and continues beside the river on the embankment. It emerges through a broken gate on to a lane. Turn right, crossing the railway by a bridge. As the lane rises again towards a second bridge, this time over the Bridgewater and Taunton Canal, turn down to the right on to the tow path.

Head along the wide, smooth path: the canal should be on your left, with the Quantock Hills rising in the distance beyond it. Half-tame swans operate on this stretch, so if you do stop to admire the Quantocks you may get pestered for your sandwich crusts.

You can also contemplate the traffic arteries of three centuries. In the 1960s the M5 motorway cut journey times between Taunton and London in half. A century before, the railway had reduced the same journey from days to hours. But the coming of the canal, earlier still, had the greatest impact: a single horse could haul the loads of 800 pack-ponies. The 18th-century engineers who oversaw the canal system brought the Industrial Revolution to Bridgwater and carried away its products.

After ½ mile (800m) you reach the **Boat and Anchor Inn**. Its bricks and tiles have moved hardly a quarter-mile from their origin in the clay pits behind. Some 50ft (15m) above its chimneypots the traffic zooms past on the M5: damaging, but not managing to destroy, the tranquil canalside

---

> **WHERE TO EAT AND DRINK** ⓘ
> The **Boat & Anchor** has outside dining (though the swans may demand a contribution) and a piano in the bar to counteract the rumble of the overhead motorway. Dogs, on leads indoors, and children are welcome.

---

scene. As you actually pass below the road, the sudden perspective of 2,000ft (600m) of concrete bridge piers is, in its way, impressive.

About ¼ mile (400m) later a small swing bridge crosses the canal at the end of **Marsh Lane**. Continue with the canal on your right. The tow path passes under the handsome brick arch of **Hamp Bridge**. Now the river and canal converge, and you can see on the opposite side the sluice where surplus canal water drains into the Parrett. On the left-hand side is a pond with many waterfowl. The tow path passes under a bridge and, after 130yds (118m), a wider one carrying the A38. Fewer than 20 paces later turn left through a gap to cross beside **Browne Pond** to a street. Turn right, continuing around the pond to a tarred path. This rises to cross the canal on another little brick bridge. Where it forks, keep to the right, to arrive at a large crossroads with traffic lights. Cross the **A39** on your left into **Taunton Road**. This leads back to the crossroads at the **Rose & Crown**, with the **Blake Museum** on the right.

> **WHAT TO LOOK FOR** ⓘ
> Beside the M5 just outside the town you may spot **Humfrey the Camel** (unless he's away doing charity work) – an escapee from a Young Farmers float in the 1982 Bridgwater Carnival. Held on the Friday after Guy Fawkes', the carnival blocks all Bridgwater's roads with the world's biggest illuminated procession.

Wiveliscombe and the Tone

A pretty village and a wooded riverside on the edge of the Brendons.

•DISTANCE•	6 miles (9.7km)
•MINIMUM TIME•	3hrs 15min
•ASCENT / GRADIENT•	1,000ft (300m) ▲▲▲
•LEVEL OF DIFFICULTY•	林 林 林
•PATHS•	Tracks, a quiet lane, a few field edges, 1 stile
•LANDSCAPE•	Wooded river valley and agricultural slopes
•SUGGESTED MAP•	aqua3 OS Explorer 128 Taunton & Blackdown Hills
•START / FINISH•	Grid reference: ST 080279
•DOG FRIENDLINESS•	Under close control in two short field sections and Marshes Lane
•PARKING•	North Street, Wiveliscombe
•PUBLIC TOILETS•	At car park

BACKGROUND TO THE WALK

Wiveliscombe formed around a crossroads that was probably more important in the Iron Age than it is today. Its earliest building is the earth fort on Castle Hill. It became quietly prosperous after Edward the Confessor gave the Manor Farm to the Bishop of Bath and Wells in the 11th century. The bishop brought in the latest monastic improvements and set up a small holiday palace for himself. It has remained prosperous ever since.

From Wool Bales to Real Ales

For most of its history Wiveliscombe has lived on wool. In the 18th century it manufactured a rough blue cloth, called Penistones, that clothed the slave population of the West Indies. Today the village has become the real ale capital of Somerset, with two separate breweries established in the late 1970s, making the Exmoor and the Cotleigh Ales. William Hancock began the first Wiveliscombe brewery in 1807. By the 1920s it was the largest brewing operation in the South West, but mergers led to its closure in 1959.

Stable Times

Wiveliscombe is away from the main roads, and also from the tourist trail, and remains largely self-sufficient: a former market town, now a local shopping centre. The town is known affectionately as Wivey, pronounced 'Wivvy'. It has moved peacefully through the centuries, almost untouched by national politics. In the 1670s the town's churchwardens were in trouble for not being nasty enough to Quakers and other nonconformists. Ten years later a survey recorded accommodation available for 76 horses and 53 human beings; the White Hart, the Bear and and the Courtyard Inn are still open for business. In 1804 the National Health Service arrived over 140 years early in the form of a free dispensary for working people and the poor.

Architectural Pot-pourri

The buildings of Wiveliscombe are a pick-and-mix of the last 1,000 years. The town hall is, sadly, boarded up; it's Victorian but looks Georgian. Opposite is an absurd building called the Court House. Technically late-Victorian, it belongs to no known architectural style, its overhanging storeys are hung with tiles and decorated with carved animal heads. In the High Street you pass between modest 18th-century terraces; the archway on the right was for stagecoaches, the one on the left may have been part of the bishop's summer palace. South Street was formerly known as 'Gullet', being the way the rainwater ran out of the town. Down in Church Street Nos 10 and 12 are timber-framed medieval cottages: No 10 has some medieval brickwork and No 12 has an upstairs windowsill that's served many centuries. The houses in Rotton Row show the local, plum-coloured sandstone. This has also been used in the 19th-century church near by and throughout the town, giving it a slightly autumnal, bruised look.

Walk 16

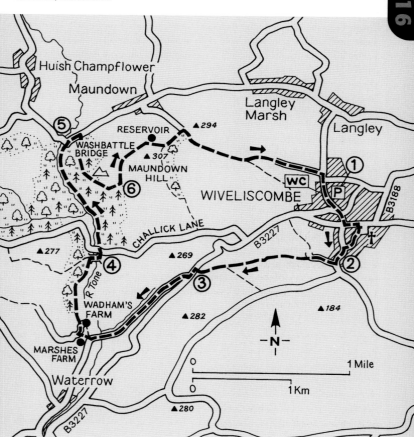

Walk 16 Directions

① Turn left out of the car park into the **Square**, head down **High Street** and turn left at the traffic lights into **Church Street**. Turn right, down some steps under an arch, to reach

Rotton Row. Continure down to **South Street** and turn left along the pavement.

② At the end of the 30mph limit turn right, into a lane, and go ahead through a gate with a footpath sign. Cross the stile ahead, and the

Walk 16

bottom edges of two large fields. Now the stile in the hedge ahead has grown over, so head up to the left for 30yds (27m) to a gateway before returning to the field foot to reach a group of farm buildings. Go up the left-hand edge of the field above to a gate on to the **B3227**.

③ Turn left, then right into a lane heading downhill. After about ¾ mile (1.2km) it crosses the **River Tone** and bends left at **Marshes Farm**. Keep ahead, on a track marked by a broken bridleway sign. Do not turn right here into the track towards **Wadham's Farm** but keep uphill to a deeply sunken lane. Turn right in this, descending towards the farm, but at its first buildings turn left. This track runs up the River Tone. With houses visible ahead, turn right at a T-junction to cross a footbridge and turn left to **Challick Lane**.

WHILE YOU'RE THERE ⓘ

The gardens at **Cothay Manor** date from 1921 – for garden design buffs, this is the Sissinghurst 'Vita Sackville West' style with garden 'rooms' in different colour schemes. They're laid around a medieval manor house (open by appointment). The gardens are open three days a week from spring to autumn. They're rather hard to find, at grid ref ST 085213 between Wiveliscombe and Wellington.

---

④ The continuing track upstream is currently beside the River Tone: a polite enquiry at the farm will let you through between its buildings. The smooth track continues upstream through very pleasant woodland to **Washbattle Bridge**.

⑤ Turn right, up the road, for 200yds (183m). A signed forest road leads uphill on the right. At the highest point of this, with a

---

WHERE TO EAT AND DRINK ⓘ

The **Bear Inn**, close to the car park, is ancient but unassuming. It serves good bar food, there is a play area for children and well-behaved dogs are welcome. Also, it offers both of the Wivey-brewed real ales.

---

pheasant fence alongside, bear left into a wide path that continues uphill. At the wood edge cross the bottom corner of a field to more woodland opposite, and turn uphill alongside this to a gate.

⑥ Go through this gate and turn left, with a hedge beside it on the left. The next gate opens on to a hedged track. This turns right, and passes a reservoir at the summit of **Maundown Hill**. At the top of a tarred public road turn sharply right into a track that becomes a descending, hedged path. At a signposted fork turn left on to a contouring path. Soon a tarred lane leads down into the town, with the car park near by on the right.

WHAT TO LOOK FOR ⓘ

Look under Washbattle Bridge and you may catch a glimpse of one of our less-known endangered species, the **white-clawed crayfish**. It's at risk of global extinction because of disease spread by the introduction of signal crayfish.

Close to the Border at the Back of Blackdown

Stapley's little valley looks down over the county boundary into Devon, towards a grim murder scene.

•DISTANCE•	3 miles (4.8km)
•MINIMUM TIME•	1hr 40min
•ASCENT / GRADIENT•	500ft (150m)
•LEVEL OF DIFFICULTY•	
•PATHS•	Field edges, and small woodland paths, 8 stiles
•LANDSCAPE•	Wooded hill slopes
•SUGGESTED MAP•	aqua3 OS Explorer 128 Taunton & Blackdown Hills
•START / FINISH•	Grid reference: ST 188136
•DOG FRIENDLINESS•	Some freedom in first, woodland, half of walk
•PARKING•	Small pull-in beside water treatment works at east end of Stapley; verge parking at walk start
•PUBLIC TOILETS•	None on route

BACKGROUND TO THE WALK

The forests of the Blackdown borders were almost the last part of Somerset to be cleared for agriculture. Here are few proper villages, just the occasional cluster of cottages around a farm. There was no obvious place for the parish church and it stands almost alone at what was once a convenient track junction. With the mechanisation of farming, the area declined again.

During the 19th century the population outside the small towns halved. Today a retired couple may occupy a cottage built for a farmworker's family of eight or a dozen people. This quiet corner of the upper Culm Valley was briefly infamous in the 1850s, when a native of this borderland became one of the last Englishmen to be hanged in public.

The Clayhidon Murder

'I think that man gathers more money than anyone else in the parish.' George Sparkes, the speaker, had just received £1 1s 5d, some butter and a drink of beer as his pay for six days of tough fieldwork in the February frost. The man he spoke of, Richard Blackmore, was a local land surveyor who had spent the day collecting tithes and taxes.

Blackmore was carrying £16 in notes and gold sovereigns – about £3,000 in today's money. The two men were drinking in the White Hart at Clayhidon until 1AM. Sparkes soon ran out of money. He tried to raise cash at cards, lost, and ended the evening owing Blackmore three pints. Drunk and resentful, he snatched a pair of blacksmith's tongs from the smithy, stalked the rent collector through the fields, and battered him to death. Some of the bloodstained sovereigns were found in his cottage the next morning.

Measures of Humanity

The trial, which took place at Exeter, was not a long one. Sparkes seemed as shocked as anyone at what he had done; but the law allowed only one sentence. It's clear that the judge was reluctant to pronounce it for so senseless a crime: he voiced the words 'to be hanged by the neck until dead' almost inaudibly, and bowed his head in tears. It is said that 10,000 people attended the hanging. The reporter for the *Exeter Flying Post* (April 1853) recorded disapprovingly the presence of women and children: 'the broadcloth of the middle classes jostling the cotton of the mechanics and labourers – a strange motley for so sad a scene and too painfully indicative of the fact that the 'lower orders' are not the only people who relish the sight of a public strangulation'.

The gallows employed the 'new drop' – a humane innovation so that the condemned man should break his neck in the fall. And the space below the trapdoor was boarded in, allowing him to die in private. The White Horse Inn has gone, but there's a memorial stone at the murder site – this is just south of a bridge over the Culm (grid ref ST 164141), at the foot of Battle Street.

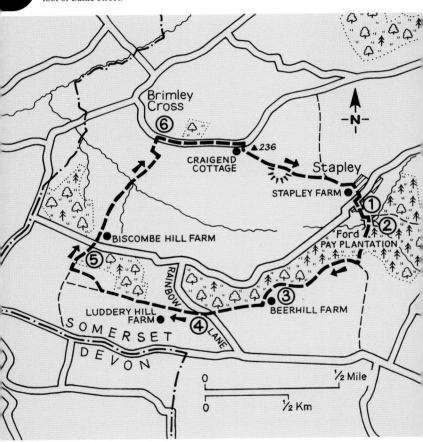

Walk 17 Directions

① A phone box marks the start of the walk. Some 20 paces below it a lane runs down between houses.

After 100yds (91m) keep ahead into a shady path. At a stile bear right to a ford with a footbridge.

② Head up a wide track. At a junction cross on to a small,

Walk 17

WHILE YOU'RE THERE

Churchstanton church has a charming setting and many interesting features. The youngest members of the party will particularly appreciate one gargoyle (the south west one on the tower). Less charming are the village stocks, of various sizes, preserved in the church porch.

waymarked path. This heads uphill, following a bank, to a stile. In the field beyond bear right, to a field corner and a stile back into woodland. A small path runs along the top edge of **Pay Plantation**, to emerge near **Beerhill Farm**.

③ Bear left for 100yds (91m) to a waymarked gate, and a second just beyond. Pass to the right of a large cowshed to reach a small pool. Pass to the right of this pool, to a gate, and follow the top edge of a wood to **Rainbow Lane**.

④ Cross the lane to a signposted stile. Pass along the left edge of a long narrow field; over on the left, **Luddery Hill Farm** is built of flinty-looking chert. A slippery stile leads into a wood of ash trees. Again the path runs along the top edge of the wood. With an isolated house visible ahead, a waymarker indicates the diverted right of way bearing right. This path slants gently downhill, to meet the driveway at a bend. Cross on to a wide path just above the driveway. At the end of the wood turn down right, to rejoin the driveway to the road below.

WHAT TO LOOK FOR

The whitish, shiny stone found in field walls and in Luddery Hill Farm is **chert**. It looks like flint, but unlike flint it comes in chunks rather than rounded nodules. The toughness of chert is one reason why the Blackdown Hills exist at all.

⑤ Cross into the trackway of **Biscombe Hill Farm**. Bear left to a field gate, and go down the right edge of a large field to a muddy hedge gap on the right. Slant down the following field to a stile at its bottom, right-hand corner, with stepping stones across the stream beyond. Go up the right-hand edge of the next field to a stile. This leads into a sunken track; turn left and follow it up to a lane.

WHERE TO EAT AND DRINK

The **York Inn** at Churchinford is a typical country hotel, with hanging baskets at the door and 15th-century beams above the open fire. It specialises in local fish and game dishes. Dogs welcome (bar only), also children (restaurant only). Alternatively, you can cross into Devon to visit the murder site and the **Merry Harriers** at Clayhidon.

⑥ Turn right, up the road. Where it levels and bends left, turn right into the driveway of **Craigend Cottage**. Turn left along field tops, with a hedge bank on your left and a view of Devon over your right shoulder. After a stile a field gate leads to a tractor track. After a short, muddy passage past **Stapley Farm** you reach the village road at the phone box.

A Walk in Prior's Park Woodlands

Prior's Park Wood is at its best with autumn's colours or spring's bluebells beautifully concealing some intricate geology.

•DISTANCE•	5 miles (8km)
•MINIMUM TIME•	2hrs 40min
•ASCENT / GRADIENT•	700t (210m) ▲▲▲
•LEVEL OF DIFFICULTY•	👫 👫 👫
•PATHS•	Rugged in Prior's Park Wood, otherwise comfortable, 7 stiles
•LANDSCAPE•	Steep, wooded slopes
•SUGGESTED MAP•	aqua3 OS Explorer 128 Taunton & Blackdown Hills
•START / FINISH•	Grid reference: ST 211182
•DOG FRIENDLINESS•	Mostly open woodland
•PARKING•	Roadside pull-off between post office and White Lion, Blagdon Hill
•PUBLIC TOILETS•	None on route

BACKGROUND TO THE WALK

Somerset is a landscape of hills that are small but steep-sided. There's a reason for this particular formation. The rocks that are now Somerset did not form until after Britain's main mountain-building episode, the collision of Scotland with England. Since then the county has been gently lifted (by the 'Africa Crunch'), but never seriously crumpled and mashed. Its rocks still lie fairly flat.

Flat Top Geology

The shape of this landscape is inextricably linked to the development of the underlying rocks. If a layer of tough rock lays fairly flat on top of much softer rocks, then where the tough rock is worn away, so the softer rocks, too, will quickly disappear. And so we end up with a flat-topped hill with a distinctive sudden edge. Such hills – at Ham Hill, at Cadbury or at Dolebury in the Mendips – proved particularly convenient for building Iron-Age forts on. The harder rock on top may be limestone – as at Glastonbury – or the greensand of the Blackdown Hills, which features on this walk.

Goyals

Small streams, such as the Curdleigh Brook seen on this walk, cut into the hard plateau rock of the Blackdown Hills, forming the little tree-lined valleys that are so typically Somerset that there's even a special Somerset word for them. 'When little boys laughed at me at Tiverton, for talking about a 'Goyal', a big boy clouted them on the head, and said that it was in Homer, and meant the hollow of the hand'; explained Jan Ridd of Exmoor, the hero of *Lorna Doone*. 'Still I know what it means well enough – to wit, a long trough among wild hills, falling towards the plain country, rounded at the bottom, perhaps, and stiff, more than steep, at the sides of it'. R D Blackmore's fictional Somerset man certainly understood the character of his county's topography.

Standing on the plateau of the Blackdown Hills, you gaze across the wide vale of Taunton at the Quantocks and Brendons. It's not too hard to see the plateau of Blackdown and the plateau of the Brendons as being part of the same ground. Indeed, this is a former ground level of 40 million years ago. But what force or process has carried away the 10 miles (16km) of scenery in between?

If all the high ground above Taunton Deane had been carried away in goyles, Blackdown should have a ragged edge rather than the straight one we see. All credit to the 19th-century geologist Sir Henry de la Beche, not for solving the problem, but for seeing that there was one to be solved. The answer lies in a process called solufluction. It still goes on today in the tundras of Alaska. In the brief, Ice-Age summer a soggy mixture of half-melted soil and slush can slip downhill over the frozen ground below. Such landslips can still be detected on the northern slopes of the Blackdown Hills, as well as in the Quantocks. They may represent the most important process which shaped today's Somerset.

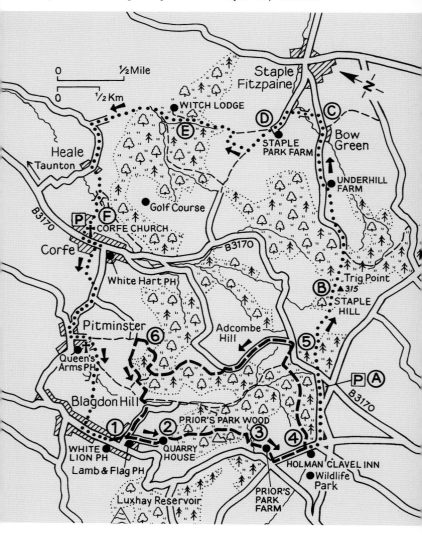

Walk 18

Walk 18 Directions

① The walk starts at the phone box opposite the **White Lion**. Cross a stile and follow the left edge of a triangular field to another stile into **Curdleigh Lane**. Cross into the ascending **Quarry Lane**. Bend left between the buildings of **Quarry House**, on to a track running up into **Prior's Park Wood**.

② From mid-April this wood is a delight with bluebells and other wild flowers. It is also fine (but possibly muddy) in late October and November. Where the main track bends left and descends slightly, keep uphill on a smaller one. This eventually declines into a muddy trod, slanting up and leftwards to a small gate at the top of the wood.

③ Pass along the wood's top edge to a gate. Red-and-white poles mark the line across the next field to another gate. After 50yds (46m) turn right, between the buildings of **Prior's Park Farm**, to its access track and a road. Turn left and follow the road with care, as it's a fairly fast section, towards the **Holman Clavel Inn**.

④ Just before the inn turn left into a forest track. Where the track ends a small path runs ahead, zig-zagging down before crossing a stream. At the wood's edge turn right up a wider path to the **B3170**.

WHAT TO LOOK FOR ⓘ
If undertaking this walk in springtime, take a wild flower identification book, as many of the woodland plants may be unfamiliar. The **early purple orchid** (flowering in early June) is one to look out for.

⑤ At once turn left on the lane signed 'Feltham'. After ½ mile (800m) a wide gateway on the left leads to an earth track. This runs along the top of **Adcombe Wood** then down inside it, giving a very pleasant descent.

WHERE TO EAT AND DRINK ⓘ
The **White Lion** at Blagdon is a handsome, 17th-century inn serving food and real ales. Families and well-controlled dogs are welcome and there is a beer garden. Blagdon Hill also has the cheerful **Lamb & Flag**, while half-way round the walk is the **Holman Clavel Inn**. Those taking Walk 19, the longer option, will find attractive inns at Corfe (the **White Hart**) and Pitminster (the **Queens Arms**).

⑥ Once below the wood follow the track downhill for 180yds (165m). Look for a gate with a signpost on the left-hand side. Go through it and follow the hedge on the right to a stile and footbridge, then bend left, below the foot of the wood, to another stile. Ignore a stile into the wood on the left, but continue along the wood's foot to the next field corner. Here a further stile enters the wood but turn right, beside the hedge, to a concrete track. Turn left – the track becomes **Curdleigh Lane**, leading back into **Blagdon Hill**.

WHILE YOU'RE THERE ⓘ
Somerset's **County Museum** is housed in Taunton Castle. Roughly 300 years ago this was the principal site of the 'Bloody Assizes'. About 500 Monmouth rebels were put on trial here: 200 of them were executed in the surrounding streets and most of the rest were transported into slavery in the West Indies. Several of their ghosts are said to haunt the building. More solidly, it houses an Iron-Age canoe which was unearthed near Glastonbury.

Blackdown Heights

An attractive longer walk to the Blackdown's highest points.
See map and information panel for Walk 18

•DISTANCE•	9¼ miles (14.9km)
•MINIMUM TIME•	4hrs 30min
•ASCENT / GRADIENT•	1,000ft (100m) ▲▲▲
•LEVEL OF DIFFICULTY•	🚶🚶 🚶🚶 🚶🚶
•START / FINISH•	Grid reference: ST 228162
•PARKING•	Large car park at Point Ⓐ; also at Point Ⓕ, Corfe church

Walk 19 Directions (Walk 18 option)

This route extends Walk 18 but starts from a high-level car park, about 750yds (686m) from the Holman Clavel Inn. From Point Ⓐ a path leads out of the back of the car park on to a minor road. Turn right and cross the **B3170** on to a track. Ignore a larger forest track on the right, but bear left through a gateway to pass through scrub to a field corner. Follow the field edge to a gate into a wood. The track rises gently: at its high point, the summit of **Staple Hill** is hidden in woods on the right, Point Ⓑ.

Follow the track down to a farm lane. At the first right bend take a field path on the right, to rejoin the lane at **Underhill Farm**. At **Bow Green** ignore a stile on the left but continue 220yds (201m) to a gate, Point Ⓒ.

Turn left across the field to a footbridge hidden in the hedge. Cross the next field near the stream on your right to another lane. Turn left for 350yds (320m), to where it bends left towards **Staple Park**

Farm, Point Ⓓ. Keep ahead into a field, and follow the bridleway up its left-hand edge. Don't go through the gate ahead, but turn right along the side of the field, and at the corner turn right again for 150yds (137m) to a narrow gate. The next gate leads on to a woodland track. This runs downhill to join the gravel access track for **Witch Lodge**, Point Ⓔ.

Where the track doubles back left, keep ahead on a downhill path. A track ahead becomes tarred and leads to a lane. Turn left for 700yds (640m) to **Heale**. Follow a track on the left for 150yds (137m), then the right edge of a field to a footbridge hidden in the hedge. A path ahead leads to **Corfe church**, Point Ⓕ.

Turn left through Corfe, to a field path on the right before a long hedge. This joins the lane into **Pitminster**. Take the lane to the church, and continue to the end of a track. Here bear right along the field edge to a footbridge, and continue under power lines to the next stile. Follow hedges on the right into **Blagdon Hill**. Continue on Walk 18 to **Holman Clavel** (Point ④). Above the inn bear left ('Frome') to the car park.

Over the Edge to Sedgemoor

From Curry Rivel to the Cider Monument for a view over the moors.

•DISTANCE•	4 miles (6.4km)
•MINIMUM TIME•	1hr 45min
•ASCENT / GRADIENT•	350ft (100m)
•LEVEL OF DIFFICULTY•	
•PATHS•	Paths, tracks and field edges, 13 stiles
•LANDSCAPE•	Wooded scarp, gentle farmland
•SUGGESTED MAP•	aqua3 OS Explorer 128 Taunton & Blackdown Hills
•START / FINISH•	Grid reference: ST 391252
•DOG FRIENDLINESS•	Mostly on leads – enclosed pasture and lanes
•PARKING•	Car park at village centre
•PUBLIC TOILETS•	None on route

Walk 20 Directions

Curry Rivel is a fairly typical Somerset village, with its mixture of small shops, pubs and stone houses, with the church rising above the tiled rooftops. Modern estates around the village have tried to blend in by using traditional building materials – and perhaps with another couple of centuries of weathering they will. 'Curry' is from the Celtic 'crwy', meaning boundary; 'Rivel' is pronounced like the end of 'arrival' and is the name of the 12th-century feudal overlord Sir Richard Revel.

Head back from the car park to turn right into the main street. Just after the **post office** a green arrow marks a high-walled path on the right. At its end turn left, in front of a trimmed yew hedge. Follow the right-hand edge of the field beyond, and cross a driveway to a stile under beech trees. The tall **Pynsent Monument** comes into sight ahead:

a 140ft (42m) waymark for the next part of your walk. It was designed by 'Capability' Brown and commemorates an act of 18th-century political sleaze. Sir William Pynsent lobbied the Prime Minister, Pitt the Elder, on behalf of the cider industry. Pitt refrained from raising the duty on cider and in gratitude Pynsent left to Pitt in his will the Burton Pynsent estate. At the time this was a perfectly respectable proceeding, and Pitt raised the column to celebrate it.

Follow a fence on the left to a stile. Ignore another stile on the left, but keep ahead towards the monument. A final stile leads on to a lane. Turn right for 170yds (155m) to a

---

WHAT TO LOOK FOR

The local blue **Lias limestone** gives Curry Rivel its rather sombre colouring. The stone weathers to a pale beige colour. In some of the buildings a mixture of dressed stone and natural, weathered faces gives a blue-and-beige, chequered effect.

Walk 20

WHERE TO EAT AND DRINK ℹ️
The **Old Forge Inn** and beer garden, at
the walk's start, has a rather classy menu
of pheasant terrine and frogs' legs – you
may feel more comfortable changing into
clean shoes in the car park first.

gateway with stone pillars. Turn left
into a field, and follow its edge
round to the right to a stile and the
Pynsent Monument with its
sudden view ahead over West
Sedgemoor.

In July 1685 the Earl of Feversham
was sent to crush the Monmouth
Rebellion. He chose a camp down
in that watery moorland, well-
protected by the many rhynes
(drainage ditches). Outnumbered
and outgunned, Monmouth staked
all on a surprise attack. In mist, at
dead of night, his pitchfork army
crept out of Bridgwater. Each man
carried a knife, with orders quietly
to stab to death the man next to
him if he made a sound. However, a
shot was fired – either by accident
or treachery. Feversham surrounded
the rebels among the rhynes. Some
200 were killed outright (against the
King's 16), and in the aftermath
many hundreds more were hanged
from the signboards of nearby inns.

Pass the monument into a dip, to
find a stile at the right-hand end of
a row of fir trees. A path leads down
through a gloomy wood. At the
bottom turn left, just inside the
wood, for 275yds (251m) to a stile
on the right. Cross open parkland,
just to the left of a pond, to a
distant gate. This leads back into
Burton Wood. Turn left, on a
tarmac track that climbs out of the
woods. Some 100yds (91m) later
comes a stile on the right; bear left
across the field corner, to a stile in
the hedge on to the **A378**. Cross

into **Moortown Lane**. This jinks
right then left to pass an orchard. It
then repeats the manoeuvre, jinking
right then left to pass a second
orchard. Here you may notice
mistletoe in the apple branches.
This parasitic plant feeds on the sap
of other trees.

Straight after this orchard turn left
through a gate. Cross the top edges
of two fields, with a wide, flat view
away to your right. A gate leads you
on to a green track. Here grows a
plant with the divided leaves of the
elder, the berries of the elder, but
clearly not the elder as it's
herbaceous, dying back in winter,
unlike a tree. It's the fairly
uncommon Danewort. The track
emerges on to **Holden's Way**. Turn
left, uphill, ignoring a side road on
the right. In another 220yds (201m)
take a stile on the right, signed
'Williton'. Follow a field edge to a
grey house with pink edges. Pass to
its left, to a gap in a tall Cupressus
hedge. An enclosed track leads out
to the **B3168**.

Turn left along the pavement, then
take the first left into **Stony Lane**.
Opposite the turn-off is Old Father
Time on a high wall above a letter
box. After 200yds (183m) take a
street on the right with an ivy-
covered wall – it leads back to
Curry Rivel's main street.

WHILE YOU'RE THERE ℹ️
Sedgemoor battlefield is a short,
signposted walk from near the
Sedgemoor Inn at Westonzoyland.
Because of its brutal aftermath the battle
lingers in the collective memory, and
many claim to have heard the cries of its
victims and the clatter of hooves drifting
through the mist. A small monument
marks the site, and the Sedgemoor Inn
has some relics of the battle.

Ilminster, the River Isle and a Walk in the Woods

A pleasing riverside ramble, an ancient village, and a wood that aspires to being ancient.

•DISTANCE•	5¾ miles (9.2km)
•MINIMUM TIME•	2hrs 40min
•ASCENT / GRADIENT•	500ft (150m) ▲ ▲ ▲
•LEVEL OF DIFFICULTY•	𝋡𝋡 𝋡𝋡 𝋡𝋡
•PATHS•	Tracks, wide paths, and riverside field edges, 12 stiles
•LANDSCAPE•	Riverside, and a small wooded hill
•SUGGESTED MAP•	aqua3 OS Explorer 128 Taunton & Blackdown Hills
•START / FINISH•	Grid reference: ST 362144
•DOG FRIENDLINESS•	Mostly on leads
•PARKING•	Pay-and-display in Ditton Street, signposted from nearby Market Cross
•PUBLIC TOILETS•	At car park

BACKGROUND TO THE WALK

These days, nothing in the countryside just happens. Fields are managed for food, although that is starting to change. Woodlands are managed for… well, it's not obvious what woodlands ought to be for. In the early Middle Ages forests were for deer, and for the men (in particular, the King) who hunted the deer. A couple of centuries later, woodlands were for pigs.

The Natural Heritage Age

Today, woods are for natural heritage. At the top of the list, this means mammals (apart from the grey squirrel, a 'baddie'), and birds. Slightly further down come butterflies, followed by woodlice, lichens and the rarer sorts of wild flowers. You don't often hear of woodlands (as opposed to commercial timber forests) being managed for the sake of the trees – perhaps that just sounds too circular. But trees too have their league table. The 'aristocrats' who can trace their lineage back to the Ice Age – oak, beech, hedge maple – are 'good'. The exception is the sycamore: the sycamore is too good at surviving, and so is considered a weed, to be eradicated. The latecomers, and other ones people may have had a hand in, are intruders; walnut and sweet chestnut are to be controlled or rooted out.

The Dog Age

Towards the bottom of the list comes the naturalist. And still important, but perhaps less so than any of the others, is the ordinary human being: the child looking for conkers, the young couple looking for privacy, the painter or photographer looking for shades of green in dappled sun, those special qualities of woodland light. I don't disagree with this: the oak and the beech are indeed handsome trees, and the spruce is gloomy. Almost all walkers are interested in wildlife. Still, why is the badger a hero but the fox a dubious character? And is it possible that, in another century or two, woodland will be managed mainly for the sake of its most enthusiastic users – our dogs? The first priorities would therefore be big piles of leaves, things that run away, and things that smell interesting when dead.

Herne Hill Wood

Assuming, then, that you're a person with an interest in wildlife (rather than a dog that just wants to chase it), in Herne Hill Wood you might spot: hazel nuts with tiny holes nibbled in them by dormice ('good!'); tree bark chewed away by the grey squirrels ('bad!'); one or two of the squirrels themselves; and you may notice the ferretty smell of badgers. Herne Hill itself was given to the people of Ilminster in 1931. Another four or five centuries should see it turning into a proper 'ancient woodland'.

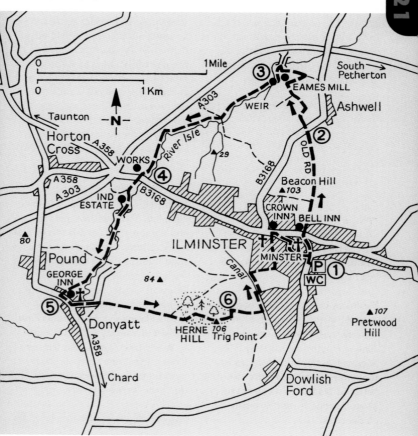

Walk 21 **Directions**

① From the car park aim for the town centre and head uphill in **North Street**. With the ancient **Bell Inn** on the left, the route continues on a path (**Old Road**). It rises past

communications equipment ancient and modern – a beacon fire-basket and then a mobile phone mast – before descending to the **B3168**.

② Cross with care into a hedged byway. Where it forks, keep right, to **Eames Mill**. Turn right, along the

Walk 21

waymarked access track. After 220yds (201m) a concrete track turns sharply back left. Just before a bridge turn left over a stile to follow the **River Isle** upstream. You have covered ¼ mile (400m) to pass from the front of **Eames Mill** to the back of the same buildings, but the rights of way don't allow a more straightforward route.

③ Cross a weir to head upstream with the river on your left. After a mile (1.6km) you'll reach the car park of the Powrmatic works, and the **B3168** beyond.

> **WHERE TO EAT AND DRINK** ⓘ
> Attractive old inns in Ilminster include the 17th-century **Bell Inn** (with a beer garden for those with four or two muddy feet) on Strawberry Bank, passed near the start of the walk, and the **Dolphin** at its end. Donyatt has the **George Inn**, with real ale and a beer garden, but no dogs allowed.

④ Cross on to a track signed 'Industrial Estate'. Pass along the river bank to the left of the buildings, and then between piles of ironwork to a footbridge back into the real world. Now with the river on your right, head upstream in a fenced way to re-cross on another footbridge. Continue over stiles along the right-hand bank. With the tower of **Donyatt church** ahead, cross diagonally right to a gate on to the road.

> **WHAT TO LOOK FOR** ⓘ
> A country-lovers' inscription from the *Book of Zephania* (Chapter III, verse i) will be found in **Donyatt church**, which is attractively built of mixed, blue and yellow limestone. The carved roof-bosses in the chancel are worth a look after you've found the 'anti-townie' quotation.

⑤ Turn left through the village, and bear left past the church. Head straight up **Herne Hill** as the lane becomes a track, then a field-edge path, then an earth path through **Herne Hill Wood**. The summit is under tall beeches. A wide avenue ahead leads to a field corner. Continue inside the wood, passing a bench and trig point on your right, and going down to the wood's foot. Here turn back left for 90yds (82m) to a gate on the right.

⑥ A wide path runs towards Ilminster, with sports fields below. Turn left, between the sports fields and the town, for 200yds (183m) to a yellow litter bin. A gap on the right leads to a path alongside a murky remnant of the **Chard-Taunton Canal**. Turn right behind tennis courts, and after 250yds (229m) turn left into **Abbots Close** and on to a tarred path. This leads to **West Street**, arriving at the **Crown Inn**. Turn right and bear right into **Silver Street**, to reach the town centre.

> **WHILE YOU'RE THERE** ⓘ
> **Barrington Court** is another of the National Trust's collection of Tudor houses in Somerset. The main interest here is the garden, laid out in the 1920s in the 'Gertrude Jekyll' style. This was a reaction against Victorian carpet-bedding into a more sophisticated version of the cottage garden. It remains the classic ideal, and a useful corrective to the fads of today's TV gardening.

Walk 22

In Praise of Lambrook's Apples

A gentle, secluded ramble around the fields and fragrant apple orchards of central Somerset.

•DISTANCE•	4¾ miles (7.7km)
•MINIMUM TIME•	2hrs 30min
•ASCENT / GRADIENT•	350ft (110m) ▲ ▲ ▲
•LEVEL OF DIFFICULTY•	🚶🚶 🚶🚶 🚶🚶
•PATHS•	Little-used field paths (some possibly overgrown by late summer), 24 stiles
•LANDSCAPE•	Fields, orchards, and a little hill
•SUGGESTED MAP•	aqua3 OS Explorer 129 Yeovil & Sherborne
•START / FINISH•	Grid reference: ST 431190
•DOG FRIENDLINESS•	Even the fiercest dog can't harm an apple tree!
•PARKING•	Street parking in East Lambrook village
•PUBLIC TOILETS•	None on route; nearest at Martock Roundabout on A303

BACKGROUND TO THE WALK

Apples were brought to Somerset by the Romans and caught on immediately. As early as the Arthur legends, Isle Avalon (Glastonbury) is the place of apples. Ten centuries later, the Normans brought the cider idea from northern France. However, even the most traditional of Somerset ciders isn't at all like the light, sparkling drink of Normandy. The real Somerset cider, known as 'scrumpy', is dark and even yeasty, lacks bubbles, and takes a bit of time to get to know. (In this it may perhaps resemble the Somerset cider drinker…)

Sheep's Nose and Brown Snout

Grape juice is already a balanced food for the yeasts of fermentation, and so is the boiled malt extract that makes beer. Squashed apples, however, are not. Sugar is needed for fermentation; tannin gives the sharpness that distinguishes real drinks from alco-pops. Sugar and tannin aren't found in the same apple, so a mixture of sweet, bitter-sweet and bitter-sour varieties is required. As many as 40 different apple varieties can go into one cider. Wonderful names have been given to these ancient cider apples: Tom Putt and Sheep's Nose have been recovered by the National Trust; Kingston Black, Yarlington Mill and Brown Snout have never gone out of favour.

Dead Rat Trick

And then, the yeast needs nitrogen, and apples don't have it. An early trick was to drop a dead rat into the cider barrel – when the rat had completely dissolved, the cider was fit to drink. (Well, obviously not fit to drink before the rat had gone…) Producers of 'real cider' won't stoop to the chemical equivalent of a rat – ammonium sulphate – so fermentation is always chancy. Even so, in spring the orchards are white with blossom from Porlock to Glastonbury. And autumn sees trailer-loads of Stokes Red and Taunton Black holding up the A303 on their way to the cider works at Shepton Mallet (smelled on Walk 35).

Like many in this part of the county, the view from Burrow Hill belies its low altitude – a mere 250ft (77m). To the south you look across a patchwork of orchards and pasture. Northwards the land drops away suddenly to the Somerset Levels. Sunset gleams in ripe-apple colours in a hundred rhynes and bits of river – even more spectacular in winter, when much of the country is flooded. Beyond the Levels, the Currys ridge rises – and here too we're looking at cider. The monument at Curry Rivel (▶ Walk 20) commemorates some parliamentary lobbying by the apple-squashers. The distillers had less reason to be grateful. Their industry was taxed to death in the 18th century for the benefit of the London gin trade. It has only recently been reborn – with results that you can sample at the foot of Burrow Hill.

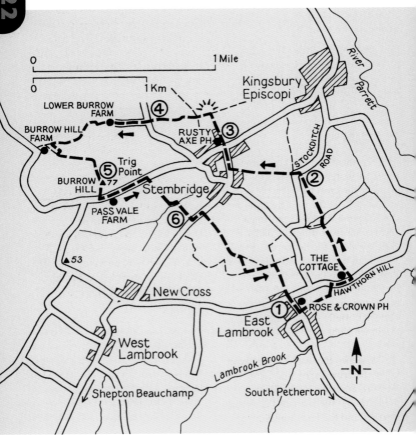

Walk 22 **Directions**

① Head into the village, turning left after 170yds (155m) on to a track. After one field a track leads left to a lane (**Hawthorn Hill**). Turn right to **The Cottage**, where a gate

with a stile leads into an orchard on the left. Follow its left edge and the following field. Cross the next field, keeping 70yds (64m) from its left edge, to a gate. Go right to a stile-with-footbridge and two long narrow orchards. At the end a gate leads on to **Stockditch Road**.

Walk 22

WHILE YOU'RE THERE

Burrow Hill Cider and the **Somerset Cider Brandy Company** are at Pass Vale Farm on the walk itself – although too much tasting of the brandy in particular may interfere with route finding over the remainder of the way. Pass Vale has the first legal licence to distil cider brandy in recorded history. The handsome copper stills, 'Josephine' and 'Fifi', are housed in Somerset's most recent 'medieval' building, erected in 2001.

② Turn left for 40yds (37m), into an overgrown track. The edge of another orchard leads to two stiles and a footbridge. Follow the left edges of two fields to a road, and turn right for 220yds (201m) to the **Rusty Axe** pub.

③ Keep ahead, on to a track that's tarred at first, past houses. On crossing the crest turn left on a green track. At the next field follow the hedge on the left (ignoring a waymarker for a different path). Halfway along the hedge, cross two stiles (can be very muddy) into a long field with the stumps of a former orchard. Keep to the left of a house to join a quiet country lane. Turn left briefly to a T-junction then turn right to pass houses.

④ Cross into the tarred driveway of **Lower Burrow Farm**, and follow waymarkers between the farm buildings. (If the farmyard is closed skirt around the farm buildings to the right.) Bear left, slanting uphill,

to a gateway. Contour across the next field to a double stile. In the next field bear right to a gate and a stile. **Burrow Hill Farm** is now just one field ahead. Turn left, up the side of this field and across its top to a gate. Go up this field to reach a row of poplars and the summit of **Burrow Hill**.

⑤ Drop to the lane at **Pass Vale Farm** and turn left for ¼ mile (400m) to a waymarked field gate on the right. Follow the left edges of two fields to a footbridge with a brambly stile. Turn left beside a stream to another brambly stile and turn right to a lane.

⑥ Turn left to a gate on the right, signed '**East Lambrook**'. Follow the left edges of three fields, then bear left over a stile and footbridge to a second bridge just beyond. In the next large field, head for the ridge slightly to your right and some farm buildings, to arrive in a small orchard. Do not cross the obvious stile out of the orchard but turn right, to its far end, where a lane leads back into **East Lambrook**.

WHAT TO LOOK FOR

Old-style **orchards** have more air and daylight. The trees are 'standards' (tall enough to walk under) and have grass below them, which is grazed by sheep. Such orchards belong to 'real cider' makers: the result is cleaner, riper apples – but fewer of them.

WHERE TO EAT AND DRINK

The 17th-century **Rose and Crown** is at the walk start and welcomes dogs; the **Rusty Axe** at Stembridge offers real ale and skittles. Good cider is near by at the **Wyndham Arms**, Kingsbury Episcopi, which is haunted by a weeping woman.

Golden Stone on the Top of Ham Hill

Ascending the hill whose warm-coloured limestone forms the towns and villages of Somerset.

•DISTANCE•	4 miles (6.4km)
•MINIMUM TIME•	2hrs
•ASCENT / GRADIENT•	700ft (210m) ▲ ▲ ▲
•LEVEL OF DIFFICULTY•	🚶 🚶 🚶
•PATHS•	Well-trodden and sometimes muddy, 5 stiles
•LANDSCAPE•	Steep-sided, wooded hill
•SUGGESTED MAP•	aqua3 OS Explorer 129 Yeovil & Sherborne
•START / FINISH•	Grid reference: ST 478167
•DOG FRIENDLINESS•	Dogs under control welcome on Ham Hill itself, may need leads elsewhere
•PARKING•	Main car park on western escarpment of Ham Hill
•PUBLIC TOILETS•	At Ranger Hut near start, and at Stoke Sub Hamden

BACKGROUND TO THE WALK

The yellow limestone, known as Hamstone, found on Ham Hill and nearby Chiseldon is of a local and special sort. Most limestone is formed of sea shells underwater, but Ham Hill was once a wave-battered, shingly bank. These well-broken shell fragments were cemented together, and stained yellow by a seepage of iron oxide, or common rust.

Consequently, the Ham Hill limestone doesn't have intact fossils. More importantly, it doesn't have the crumbliness of most limestones, or the tendency to split apart into layers. It's what is called 'freestone' – it can be worked smooth and carved in any direction. Shaping Hamstone is like cutting cheese rather than flaky pastry.

Romans in the Stone

Traces of early quarrying naturally get dug up and carried away by later quarrying. However, we do know that the Romans quarried here: a Roman coffin made of Ham Hill stone is in the museum at Dorchester. However, it was much later, in the Middle Ages, that the quarries became the making of Somerset – literally. The more important buildings – Montacute House at the foot of the hill, but also Sherborne Abbey, Wells Cathedral and many manor houses – were built of Hamstone throughout.

Shop Local

Because of the cost of hauling the stones, in the days before real roads, buildings such as parish churches used the local stone for masonry but Hamstone for the corners and the tricky bits round the windows. The Yeo and the Parrett provided river transport, and Hamstone could be floated up the Tone to Taunton and Wellington. All over Somerset it's a golden thread running through the richly varied building fabric. Another quality of Hamstone is apparent at Bath, where they had their own sort of freestone and didn't need to use it. The Bathstone, an oolitic limestone, is crumbling in today's polluted atmosphere. The

Hamstone, a sort of natural concrete, is more robust. The quarries were worked by hand, using wedges and a type of pick called a 'jadd'. The tremendous labour of lifting the rough-shaped blocks out of the quarries was a spur to ingenuity and mechanical contrivance. Steam-powered cranes came to Ham Hill in the 18th century but, even so, the work was dangerous, with quarrymen injured or crushed to death every year.

Back to the Future

Today two of the quarries have re-opened. They are being worked in the traditional way, with wedges and hand tools. The fork-lift truck provides a safer alternative to the block-and-tackle or steam crane. The stone goes for restoration work and also for new building. Cheap transport in the 20th century meant stone for a fancy façade could come from Spain or even China, but today planners are realising that the local stone is crucial to Somerset's character and charm.

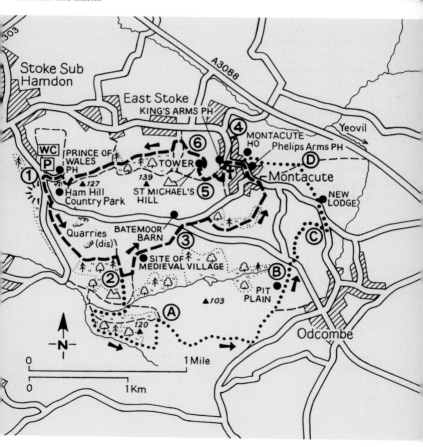

Walk 23 **Directions**

① Turn right out of the car park (so that the big, westward view is on the right) and follow the road to a junction. Bear left for 35yds (32m) then take a path on the right, signed 'Norton Sub Hamdon'. This leads through woods around the side of **Ham Hill**, keeping at the same level, just below the rim, all the way round. When open field appears ahead, turn right, downhill. Ignore a first gate on the left and continue to a second.

② Descend grassland into a small valley with the hummocks of the medieval village of **Witcombe**. Head up the valley floor, passing to the left of a willow clump. A grassy path climbs the right-hand side of the valley to a field corner. Here turn left on a track that leads to a lane near **Batemoor Barn**.

③ **Hollow Lane** descends directly opposite. A stile just to its right lets you pass along the field edges, then into a wood. Just twenty paces on, turn right to a stile. A clear path runs just below the top of the wood, then down to the edge of **Montacute** village. Turn left near the entrance to **Montacute House**, to reach the **King's Arms** inn.

④ Turn left, past the church; after a duck pond turn right on a permissive path. A kissing gate leads to the base of **St Michael's Hill**. Turn left for 150yds (139m) to a stile into the woods.

⑤ The path ahead is arduous. For a gentler way up the hill, turn left

---

WHILE YOU'RE THERE ⓘ

Montacute House is one of the finest Elizabethan houses in the country. There's a back view on Walk 24; this may well tempt you to pay the National Trust's entry fee to get a proper look. Nearby **Tintinhull** (also National Trust) has a much more modest house in a small but intensely colourful garden.

---

around its base to meet the descending track. Otherwise head slightly left up a very steep path, to join the same track just below the summit **tower**. The tower is open and its spiral staircase is well worth the climb. Descend the spiralling track to the gate at the hill's foot.

⑥ Turn half-right and go straight down the field to a gate that leads on to a track corner. Turn left and follow the track round the field corner. After 90yds (82m) take a right fork. The earth track runs close to the foot of the woods, passing the ruins of a pump house, and diminishing to a path; it then climbs steps to join a higher one. Turn right to continue close to the foot of the woods until the path emerges at a gate after 500yds (457m). Steps lead up to the **Prince of Wales** pub. Turn left along its lane, passing through the hummocks of former quarries, to the car park.

WHAT TO LOOK FOR ⓘ

The outdoor tables of the Prince of Wales give a clear view of medieval **strip lynchets** on the hillside. Where valley bottoms were boggy, the well-drained hill slopes were best for cultivation. Strip lynchets were a system of terracing so that at least part of the slope would be gentle enough to cultivate.

WHERE TO EAT AND DRINK ⓘ

The **Prince of Wales**, Ham Hill, is very much a walker's pub. It welcomes dogs and even muddy boots. The view over half of Somerset is just as good to sit at with a drink as it is to walk past. The pub is closed on Mondays in the off-season. Montacute has two attractive old inns, the **Phelips Arms** and the **King's Arms**.

Ham and Odcombe

A longer ramble, adding High Wood to Ham Hill with unexpected views of Montacute House.

See map and information panel for Walk 23

•DISTANCE•	6½ miles (10.4km)
•MINIMUM TIME•	3hrs 15min
•ASCENT / GRADIENT•	800ft (240m) ▲ ▲ ▲
•LEVEL OF DIFFICULTY•	👣 👣 👣

Walk 24 Directions (Walk 23 option)

At Point ② of the previous walk keep ahead down the fairly steep, sunken path to a track at the foot of the wood. Cross to a kissing gate and bear right to a gate into **High Wood**. A path under laurels works its way round the hill, rising gently at first. After ¼ mile (400m) it bends left, around the hill: here ignore waymarked side-paths down right and up left. The path works its way right round the hill to emerge into an open field. Keep ahead for 40yds (37m) to a fence and turn up alongside it, following it across the face of the hill and down to a kissing gate and the track below, Point Ⓐ.

Turn right for ¾ mile (1.2km) to a T-junction near a road. Turn left and after ¼ mile (400m) keep ahead rather than forking right into **Odcombe**. The track joins the tarred driveway of **Pit Plain** farm. Bear right to a lane, Point Ⓑ.

Cross to a field gate and track, to take a stile on the left just before a walled graveyard. At the next corner of the graveyard bear right over another stile, and go down a path into a wooded hollow ahead. The path bears up the right-hand side of the hollow, to a fenced path and a stile. Turn right, around the slope with a fence just below, passing three sheds to a field gate. Two more gates immediately below lead down to a road, Point Ⓒ.

Follow this lane to the left to join a larger road, and keep ahead on this to the imposing gateway of **New Lodge**. Go through the gates on to a gravel track under a fine avenue of oaks. At its end, **Montacute House** appears ahead in an unexpected back view. This is Point Ⓓ.

Here turn down left to a waymarked stile with dog slot. Note the direction of the waymarking arrow here: it points towards **Montacute church** and **St Michael's Tower** above. At the far side of the field is a small gate (the field boundary being a fence to the right of this gate and a hedge to its left): this leads into the formal gardens of **Montacute House**. Keep ahead, through three arched gateways, then turn left to the lodge and the main street of the village, with the **King's Arms** up to the right. Continue on Walk 23 picking up at Point ④.

Surviving the Reformation in Winsham and Wayford

A walk between two remarkable villages, featuring two very different churches, hidden in the chalk combes of south west Somerset.

•DISTANCE•	7 miles (11.3km)
•MINIMUM TIME•	3hrs 30min
•ASCENT / GRADIENT•	900t (270m) ▲▲▲
•LEVEL OF DIFFICULTY•	🚶 🚶 🚶
•PATHS•	Byways, tracks (some tarred), minor roads, field edges, 2 stiles
•LANDSCAPE•	Gently rolling hills
•SUGGESTED MAP•	aqua3 OS Explorer 116 Lyme Regis & Bridport
•START / FINISH•	Grid reference: ST 375063
•DOG FRIENDLINESS•	Dogs can be off leads along byways
•PARKING•	Street parking near Bell Inn
•PUBLIC TOILETS•	None on route

Walk 25 Directions

Winsham is a lovely village, with houses in Mediterranean colours of yellow and pink as well as the golden Hamstone. Winsham church is essentially medieval. This is because after 1550 official Protestantism under Edward VI saw much church decoration removed or destroyed. For the rest of that century each new monarch had the old vicar removed for having the 'wrong' religion. Understandably, the wealthy stopped leaving their

money to the church and left it to their descendants instead – the grand buildings of Tudor and Stuart times were not churches but country houses.

At the foot of Winsham's main street turn left into **Court Street**, with a footpath sign for Wayford. The path becomes a track. Where another track crosses, keep ahead into a field, to pass to the right of **Broadenham Farm** with its handsome Hamstone porch. Follow waymarkers between the farm buildings to a lane. Turn right and follow the lane to **Hey Farm**. Waymarkers lead round to the right of the buildings. Ignore two tracks on the left as the main track bends to the right. Follow it through **Ashcombe Farm** – although the right of way diverts to the left, the track between the buildings is a permitted path. In another ½ mile (800m) you reach the parking area at the foot of **Wayford Wood**.

WHILE YOU'RE THERE

Forde Abbey isn't among Somerset's superb collection of early country houses – it's actually 150yds (137m) into Dorset. A medieval abbey, transformed in 1649, it has one of the finest and most varied selections of ceilings in the country. The gardens are also magnificent, with many water features including the former moat.

Walk 25

WHAT TO LOOK FOR
This is a **chalk landscape**. Chalk is porous, so the hillsides have no goyals (little stream valleys). Valleys did form in the Ice-Age summers, when streams flowed but the underground was frozen. Those former waterways have now smoothed out, and the result today is a gently rolling scene. After Chalkway you cross a chalk stream with its flinty bed.

Go through a gate to a noticeboard with a map. Turn right, passing to the right of a wooden building, and go up the main path. With the wood edge visible above on the left, the path bends to the right; take a left fork to pass a bench, dated 1987, and date palms. The path crosses the top of the wood for 220yds (201m) then turns downhill again, eventually emerging down steps on to the track below the wood. Turn left for ¼ mile (400m) into **Wayford**. A golden manor house, a few stone cottages and a tiny church make up the village of Wayford, with just a single road leading out to the rest of the world. Keep ahead to the chapel, barely bigger than a room. In this small, undecorated space, you might feel God is sitting right beside you. (You can divert through the churchyard to rejoin the lane beyond.)

At the end of the village, at 'Give Way' markings, turn left up the steep and hedged **Chard Lane**. At the top of the hill, opposite a road designated 'Unsuitable for Motors', turn left through an unmarked gate. Take a faint green track out across the field, to a single oak tree where a hedge runs down to the right. Go past the oak and along the hedge behind to a gate into a farm track. After 100yds (91m) the track bends left: here climb a gate ahead and follow the hedge on your right to the field corner and a gate into a lane. Turn right for 220yds (201m) then left into a concrete farm track signposted for Chalkway. The track leads through **Midnell Farm** and then **Lue Farm**, where it passes through a large shed. After ¼ mile (400m) it joins a road.

Turn left, down into a gloomy wood of larches, and then right, over a cattle grid, on to a tarred track. This runs through parkland, to reach a lane. Turn left, down over a mossy bridge, over the crest of a hill, and down towards Winsham. Just above the village a stile on the left is signed for **Back Street**. Cross a field corner to pass to the left of some houses. Another stile leads into the village: turn downhill to reach the **Bell Inn**, but be sure to visit the church before you leave.

WHERE TO EAT AND DRINK
The **Bell** at Winsham serves home-made pies and real ales. Dogs (on leads) are welcome but muddy boots aren't; however, there is an outdoor eating area. The church is opposite.

Winsham church is unusual for having retained its rood screen. This carved partition between the congregation and the altar was particularly objectionable to the Protestant style-police. Even more remarkable is the painted tympanum, the wooden panel that filled the space above the screen. This 14th-century crucifixion scene lay under whitewash throughout the Reformation and it was not rediscovered until Victorian times. We are so accustomed to the Victorian-piety style of religious painting – pale people, eyeballs rolled heavenwards – that this down-to-earth painting comes as a refreshing shock.

Coneygore Hill and Cucklington

Up and down the hill in deepest Somerset, taking in a church with over a thousand years of history.

•DISTANCE•	5½ miles (8.8km)
•MINIMUM TIME•	2hrs 45min
•ASCENT / GRADIENT•	600ft (180m) ▲ ▲ ▲
•LEVEL OF DIFFICULTY•	🚶 🚶 🚶
•PATHS•	Little-used field paths, which may be overgrown, 11 stiles
•LANDSCAPE•	Small hills grazed by cows
•SUGGESTED MAP•	aqua3 OS Explorer 129 Yeovil & Sherborne
•START / FINISH•	Grid reference: ST 747298
•DOG FRIENDLINESS•	Route over pasture so on leads or under close control
•PARKING•	Lay-by on former main road immediately south of A303
•PUBLIC TOILETS•	None on route

BACKGROUND TO THE WALK

Throughout the Middle Ages sheep brought increasing prosperity to Somerset. And the merchants, spinners and clothiers could think of no better way to spend their wool money than in glorifying God. With the monasteries becoming ever richer and less religious, the good Somerset yeoman preferred to praise God and improve his village by making a donation to his parish church.

Somerset Churches
So, in every corner of the county, in the Norman style or in the sturdy simplicity of the English Gothic, there rose the church towers of Somerset. By the end of the 12th century there were nearly 500 of them – 21 of our 50 walks involve a church. The towers of yellow limestone rose above thatched villages, cornfields and green fields. They provided waymarkers for wanderers among the ditches and reed beds. The church ale, or fund-raising party, was the main social event of the village. ('Ale' is an archaic word for festival, at which this liquor was drunk.)

Early English and Decorated
The Norman style of church is recognisable by its round arches. Few such churches have survived in England. Many of the later churches, including Cucklington, retain their Norman font. The Early English is the beginning of the Gothic, pointy-arch style. The windows are single and narrow, called 'lancets'. Interior decoration often uses the polished, pale-grey limestone from Dorset known as Purbeck marble. Wells Cathedral, with its ornate front and breathtaking inverted arch is the crowning glory of the Early English style. The Gothic was essentially a new way of building stone structures that didn't fall down. As the builders got more skilful, they were able to leave out more of the stone. From about 1300, the style called Decorated has compound windows, in three or five panels, like the west window at Cucklington.

Somerset has few Perpendicular churches; a rare example is seen in St Barbara's Chapel in Cucklington. Here, in stained glass, you can see St Barbara herself, patron saint of hills – she is shown locked up in a tower by her heathen papa. In fact Cucklington church was built and rebuilt over several centuries – study it closely and it's a history of the last thousand years. St Barbara's Chapel was a chantry, where prayers were said for some rich benefactor. Around 1500 such short-cuts to heaven were deemed unseemly, and the chapel was incorporated into the body of the church. Unfortunately the people in the chapel couldn't see the priest, so they built the peculiar peephole that's called a hagioscope or squint. The church owes its feeling of space and simplicity to the wrecking activities of the Puritans. There is a colourful and enthusiastic royal coat of arms, painted at the restoration of Charles II. The roof was put back on again after the great storm of 1705.

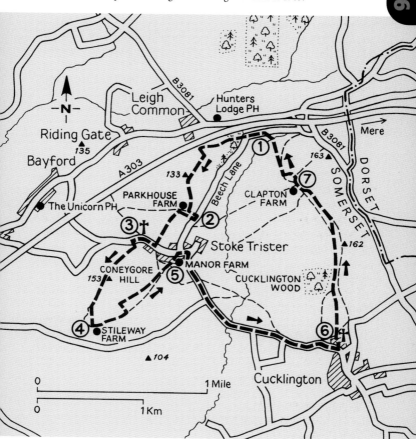

Walk 26 Directions

① With your back to the A303, walk right along the lane to where a track runs ahead into a wood. At its far side a fenced footpath runs alongside the main road. Turn left up a path, then right into a fenced-off path that bends round to the left to reach **Parkhouse Farm**. After an uncomfortably nettly passage (in summer) to the left of the buildings, turn again left to a lane.

Walk 26

WHERE TO EAT AND DRINK ⓘ
The **Hunters' Lodge** at Leigh Common is an A303 roadhouse. The attractive **Unicorn** at Bayford is an earlier version, a 270-year-old coaching inn (no bar meals on Mondays; no children's licence; dogs welcome).

② Turn back right, to follow the field edge back alongside the farm track. Go through a gate and at once turn left through a field gate. Aiming towards **Stoke Trister church**, follow the left edge of one field and then go straight up a second, turning right along a lane to reach the church.

WHAT TO LOOK FOR ⓘ
Rabbits… Coneygore, or 'Coneygar', is a rabbit warren. Rabbits were introduced by the Normans as a convenience food; just dig them out a bank to burrow into, and send two men with a ferret and a net at dinner time.

③ Continue for 170yds (155m) to a stile. Go uphill past a muddy track, but turn right alongside the hedge immediately above. Follow this around **Coneygore Hill**, over one stile, to a second one; then go straight down to **Stileway Farm**.

④ Turn left by the top of the farm buildings. Continue into a field track but at once take a gate above, and pass along the base of two fields, to a gate by a cattle trough. Head uphill, with the hedge now on your left, to the steeper bank around **Coneygore Hill**. Turn right

WHILE YOU'RE THERE ⓘ
With this walk so handy for the A303, it might be appropriate to take in the **Haynes Motor Museum** at Sparkford. The Model J Duesenberg Tourer is worth $1,000,000, the Sinclair C5 and Prince Harry's go-kart rather less.

and follow this banking to a stile. Keep on to a gap between bramble clumps and then slant down right to a gate in the corner. This leads on to a green track and then to a lane near **Manor Farm**.

⑤ Turn downhill past a thatched cottage and a red phone box, and bear right for **Cucklington**. There are field paths on the left, but it's simpler to use this lane to cross the valley and climb to Cucklington village. A gravel track on the left leads to **Cucklington church**.

⑥ Pass to the left of the church, and contour across two fields, passing above **Cucklington Wood**. In the third field slant up to the right to join a track, which leads to **Clapton Farm**.

⑦ After the Tudor manor house the track bends right, uphill. Turn left between farm buildings to a gate, and then turn left again down a wooded bank. Turn right, along the base of the bank, to a gap in a grown-out hedge. Now bear left past a power pole to the field's bottom corner. Cross two small streams and bear left to cross a third stream and a stile beyond. Go straight up to a stile by a cattle trough and the lane you parked on.

Cadbury Castle as Camelot?

A hill fort gives wide views of Somerset and a glimpse of pre-history.

•DISTANCE•	6¾ miles (10.9km)
•MINIMUM TIME•	3hrs 30min
•ASCENT / GRADIENT•	1,000ft (300m) ▲▲▲
•LEVEL OF DIFFICULTY•	👫 👫 👫
•PATHS•	Well-used paths, 6 stiles
•LANDSCAPE•	Steep-sided, green hills
•SUGGESTED MAP•	aqua3 OS Explorer 129 Yeovil & Sherborne
•START / FINISH•	Grid reference: ST 632253
•DOG FRIENDLINESS•	Mixed farming: some fields under crops, reasonable freedom
•PARKING•	Cadbury Castle car park (free), south of South Cadbury
•PUBLIC TOILETS•	None on route

BACKGROUND TO THE WALK

Cadbury Castle was a military stronghold for over 4,000 years. The ditches and earth walls first rose in the Stone Age, and were extended in the Bronze Age. In the Iron Age it became the capital of the Durotinges tribe, who gave their name to Dorset. Here they built a town of wood, willow-wattle and thatch and held out against the Romans. The Romans won in the end: they burnt down the hilltop town in around AD 70.

The Saxon, Ethelred the Unready, repaired the fort against the Vikings. Again it became a wartime capital, replacing Ilchester between 1009 and 1019. Coins were minted here, and labelled 'CADANBYRIC'.

King Arthur in Somerset

The local belief that Cadbury is indeed King Arthur's Camelot was first recorded in 1542 – more than 1,000 years after King Arthur. However, it was supported by excavations in the 1960s, which showed that, at the very time of the legendary King Arthur, the walls were rebuilt in timber and stone. Some of this stonework is visible on the left as you return to the track down off the hill. A large and kingly timber hall rose on the hilltop. Finds of pottery imported from the eastern Mediterranean indicate a place of wealth and good taste.

In this wooden hall the various strands of legend converge. We can imagine rich tapestries hanging from the panelled walls, and below them the court intrigues and amours, described by the 15th-century Sir Thomas Malory. It's even easier to see Queen Guenevere and her ladies riding out along Corton Ridge to gather may-blossom. But at the end of a short mid-winter's day, in the darkness under the trees, the pre-Christian, holly-bearing Green Knight of the anonymous Gawain Poet comes striding up the long earthen ramp. And if he did exist, it was very possibly from here that Arthur and his knights went forth to the battle of Mons Badonis, which may have been at Bath, to conquer the Saxon; and later to defeat at the bloody battle of Camlann.

Like most of the limestone hillocks of Somerset that made such fine forts, Cadbury has a wide view over the Levels. The viewpoint cairn was raised at the Millennium; in accordance with the Arthurian environment, the places indicated are mostly mystic and invisible. The eye of faith and legend sees behind the horizon to Stonehenge, Avebury and Tintagel. But in winter, the actual eye can trace the possible route of Arthur's final journey, through the flooded fields of the Somerset Levels. Legend would have it that three queens in a black barge carried him through the high water to Glastonbury, on Avalon Isle, knowing his wound was a deadly one. And there he supposedly rests, hidden in the hill, waiting for Britain's hour of need.

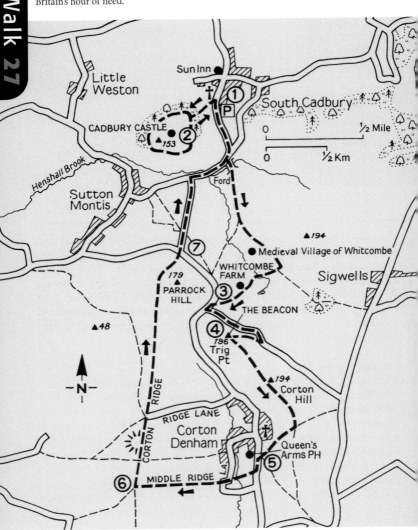

Walk 27 Directions

① Turn right out of the car park to the first house in South Cadbury. A stony track leads up on to **Cadbury Castle**. The ramparts and top of the fort are access land, so you can stroll around at will.

② Return past the car park. After ¼ mile (400m) you pass a side road

Walk 27

WHERE TO EAT AND DRINK

The **Queen's Arms** at Corton Denham is on the walk route and has a walkers' bar. My own favourite, however, is the **Mitre** at Sampford Orcas, which has good food and guest ales, and welcomes dogs and well-behaved children. The **Sun** at South Cadbury is also near by.

on the left, to reach a stile marked 'Sigwells'. Go straight down to a stile and footbridge. Follow the left edge of a field and then an uncultivated strip. A track starts ahead, but take a stile on the right to follow the field edge next to it, to a gate with two waymarkers. A faint track leads along the top of the following field. At its end turn down into a hedged earth track. This leads out past **Whitcombe Farm** to rejoin the road.

③ Turn left to a junction below **Corton Denham Beacon**. Turn left to slant uphill for ¼ mile (400m). A short green track on the right leads on to the open hilltop and the summit trig point.

④ Head along the steep hill rim to a stile with a dog slot. Continue along the top of the slope, with Corton Denham below. You pass a modern 'tumulus', a small, covered reservoir. Above five large beeches slant gently down to a waymarked gate. A green path slants down again, until a gate lets you on to a tarred lane; follow this until you reach the road below.

⑤ Turn left on the road, which is narrow between high banks, for 110yds (100m) to a stile marked 'Middle Ridge Lane'. Keep to the left of the trees to a field gate, with a stile beyond leading into a lane. Go straight across into a stony track that climbs gently to the ridgeline.

⑥ Turn right, and walk along **Corton Ridge** with a hedge on the right and a wide view on the left. After 650yds (594m) **Ridge Lane** starts on the right, but go through a small gate on the left to continue along the ridge. After a small gate a green path bends around the flank of **Parrock Hill**. With Cadbury Castle now on the left, ignore a first green track down to the left. Soon afterwards the main track itself turns down left into a hedge end and waymarked gate. A hedged path leads down to a road.

⑦ Cross into a road signed 'South Cadbury'. After 700yds (640m) turn right, again for South Cadbury, and follow the road round the base of **Cadbury Castle** to the car park.

WHILE YOU'RE THERE

The modern equivalent of King Arthur's knights are the jets and helicopters at **Yeovilton**. This naval air station is one the busiest airfields in Britain. Within the Royal Navy, such stations are referred to as if they were ships: Yeovilton is HMS *Heron*. After watching from Corton Ridge, you may be interested to visit Yeovilton's noisy **Fleet Air Arm Museum**.

WHAT TO LOOK FOR

From the Somerset hills with their wide views, **signal fires** carried news of the Spanish Armada. In Blackmore's *Lorna Doone* the fire on Dunkery Beacon warned of the Doones out raiding (at least until the night when the Doones threw the signalman into his own fire). Above Ilminster the fire-basket still stands on the hill. Corton Hill has a view across the Levels to Brent Knoll and even to Wales. However, the red glare from Corton Beacon now is a warning for aircraft at Yeovilton. The summit also has a trig point and a stone shelter bench.

Walk 28

Edge of the Levels

From Polden's edge down on to the Somerset Levels and up again.

•DISTANCE•	4½ miles (7.2km)
•MINIMUM TIME•	2hrs 15min
•ASCENT / GRADIENT•	450ft (140m) ▲ ▲▲
•LEVEL OF DIFFICULTY•	🚶🚶 🚶🚶 🚶🚶
•PATHS•	Initially steep then easy tracks and paths, 3 stiles
•LANDSCAPE•	Water-meadows of the Somerset Levels, and wooded heights above
•SUGGESTED MAP•	aqua3 OS Explorer 141 Cheddar Gorge
•START / FINISH•	Grid reference: ST 480345
•DOG FRIENDLINESS•	Off leads on drove tracks and in woods
•PARKING•	Car park (free) at Street Youth Hostel, just off B3151; another car park on south side of road
•PUBLIC TOILETS•	None on route; nearest are at Street

BACKGROUND TO THE WALK

Of Somerset's six hill ranges, the Poldens are the smallest; they rise to just 390ft (119m) at Great Breach Wood. Along the hedged A39 the car driver won't have any feeling of being on a summit ridge. The passengers, however, will be getting glimpses, between the branches, of wide lands on either side. And if you get out and stand at the top of the southern scarp, the long, windswept edge above the Levels is almost like the top of a sea cliff. In fact, a sea cliff is what it once was. The Bristol Channel has flowed over the Levels several times in the last few millennia – and still does, occasionally, during winter floods. To the north, the village of Burtle stands not on peat but on a sandbank with seashells. Glastonbury Tor and Brent Knoll were formed as islands undercut by the waves.

Hardy's Tragic Poem

This high, dry ridge has been a road since Roman times. An inn stood at Marshall's Elm, now the site of the Street Youth Hostel and the start of our walk. An incident here provoked Thomas Hardy (1840–1928) to put pen to paper. *A Trampwoman's Tragedy* (1902) concerns flirtation and murder, and was turned down by the editor of *Cornhill* magazine in the United States as 'not a poem he could possibly print in a family periodical'. Despite being set in Somerset, Hardy considered it his most successful poem – and much shorter than any of the Dorset novels.

> 'And as the sun drew down to west,
> We climb the toilsome Polden crest,
> And saw, of landskip sights the best,
> The inn that beamed thereby.
> Beneath us figured tor and lea,
> From Mendip to the western sea –
> I doubt if finer sight there be
> Within this royal realm.'

Given the Polden range's status as a former sea cliff, it's quite appropriate that one of England's admirals should stand on Windmill Hill, in the shape of a stone column. Samuel Hood, who was born in 1724, is perhaps England's seventh most famous admiral. He entered the navy as a teenager, and rose to distinguish himself as a bad-tempered but effective commander. American historians seem relieved that, during the Battle of the Capes in Chesapeake Bay in 1781, a bad decision by Admiral Rodney left Hood a bystander while the Royal Navy suffered one of its worst-ever defeats.

In the early part of the Napoleonic War, Hood served in the Mediterranean. He mounted a successful raid on Toulon in 1793; a junior officer on the raiding party, one Horatio Nelson, was wounded by flying gravel thrown up by a cannonball and lost the sight in one eye. Hood retired the next year, and died in 1814 after seeing his tactical ideas triumphantly continued by young Nelson.

Walk 28

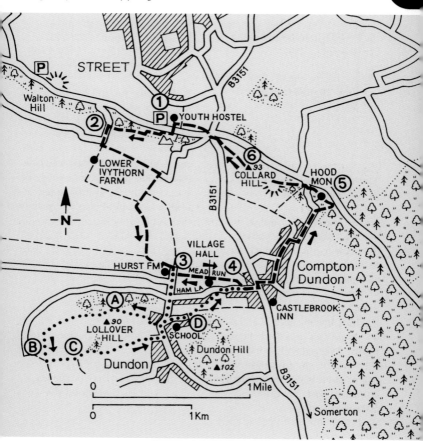

Walk 28 Directions

① From the parking area on the youth hostel side, cross and turn right on a woodland path. After

100yds (91m) a smaller path descends on the left by steps. At the foot of the wood turn right, and at a field corner go down a little to a track. This runs along the base of the wood to a lane.

Walk 28

② Go down to the entrance to **Lower Ivythorn Farm**, and turn left into a track. After ½ mile (800m) this reaches the corner of an unsurfaced road, where you turn right. After ¼ mile (400m) the track turns left into a field. Follow its edge, with a ditch and fence to your left, to a gate. In the next field continue alongside the ditch to the corner. The former footbridge is derelict under brambles. Take a gate on the left, then turn right on a field track. This zig-zags to pass to the left of **Hurst Farm**, leading to a tarred lane.

> **WHILE YOU'RE THERE** ⓘ
>
> From the Middle Ages onwards, the affluence and development of the Levels was signalled by the number of windmills along the Polden ridge. **Stembridge Tower Mill** at High Ham is more recent, dating from 1822. It has been restored by the National Trust, though not yet into full working order.

③ Turn right to a bridleway sign on the left. Follow this green track until it joins **Ham Lane**. This leads to the crossroads of the **B3151** in Compton Dundon, with the Castlebrook Inn down to the right.

④ Cross the busy B3151 and pass between an ancient market cross (right) and an ugly Victorian obelisk (left) into **Compton Street**. At the first junction keep round to the left, towards the **Hood Monument** above. As the street starts to climb, turn right and left up the lane beyond. Where it reaches woodland turn off through a waymarked gate signed 'Reynolds Way'. The path slants up into the wood. Then, some 35yds (32m) before it arrives at a road, turn left along the top of the steep ground, to the Hood Monument.

> **WHERE TO EAT AND DRINK** ⓘ
>
> The **Castlebrook Inn** in Compton Dundon is a short distance from Point ④. This old coaching inn welcomes dogs and children, and serves bar meals and real scrumpy cider.

⑤ Continue down through the wood to a minor road, with the main road 50yds (46m) away on the right. Ignore a path descending opposite but turn right for a few steps to a footpath sign and a kissing gate. A grass path heads gently up the crest of **Collard Hill**, with wide views to the left.

⑥ From the summit go straight on down to a stile and the signposted crossroads of the **B3151**. Cross both roads. The ridge road is signposted for the youth hostel, and your path is just to its right. It crosses a glade into woodland. Keep to the right of some hummocky ground to the wood's edge, and follow this path to the car park.

> **WHAT TO LOOK FOR** ⓘ
>
> The medieval **market cross** passed in Compton Dundon is of yellow Hamstone, its edges softened by the weathering of the centuries. The **obelisk** is of imported granite, polished to a hard shine that will never weather.

Loll Over Lollover Hill

A Polden outlier, ideal for picnics and for viewing the surrounding ranges.
See map and information panel for Walk 28

•DISTANCE•	7 miles (11.3km)
•MINIMUM TIME•	3hrs 30min
•ASCENT / GRADIENT•	850ft (290m) ▲ ▲ ▲
•LEVEL OF DIFFICULTY•	狀 狀 狀
•DOG FRIENDLINESS•	English Nature asks that dogs be on leads within SSSI

Walk 29 Directions (Walk 28 option)

This simple round of Lollover Hill can be done as an extension to Walk 28, or as a self-contained short walk (3 miles/4.8km), starting from the village hall on Ham Lane.

From **Hurst Farm** (Point ③ on Walk 28) carry straight on down the access road to cross **Ham Lane** into **Dundon** village. The street bends right and then sharply left. Just after this corner earth steps lead up on the right, with a waymarker for **Lollover Hill** (wrongly marked as ¼ mile, in fact closer). Pass between hedges to an earth track, and turn right. The track bends left and heads uphill, with the church tower emerging from woodland behind. A stile leads into the Site of Special Scientific Interest (SSSI) around **Lollover** summit, Point Ⓐ.

The track runs by a wood on the right, with the trig point on the left. The track reaches another stile and gate at the end of the SSSI. After another stile follow the hedge ahead, walking on its left. Cross another stile, ignore a stile and footbridge on the right, and continue down the spur to yet another stile. The hedge now bends left to a gate, Point Ⓑ.

Cross the top edge of the field beyond, to a gate with a stile on the left. Go through this and walk along the next field, 30yds (27m) out from its right-hand hedge, to a stile over an electric fence leading to a track corner, Point Ⓒ. Walk up through a wood, then between hedges. It descends to become a lane into **Dundon**.

Turn left up the village street, go round the sharp right-hand bend and fork right past the school (Point Ⓓ). Where the lane ends, a track runs ahead. After 60yds (55m) take a gate on the left, and follow the church path – a half-buried line of flagstones along the field edge. Take a gate on the left and turn right, still on flagstones, to cross the corner of a field into a small wood. The path passes between steadings, through three more gates. Cross a final field diagonally left to a gate leading out on to **Ham Lane** near the village hall.

To continue on Walk 28 turn right, noting in the verge the continuing flagstones of the church path. The lane reaches the **B3151** at Point ④.

Medieval Marketing and Geology at Glastonbury

Legend, geology and architecture combined: King Arthur, a sacred thorn, a Somerset tor and ten centuries of fine buildings.

•DISTANCE•	2½ miles (4km)
•MINIMUM TIME•	1hr 30min
•ASCENT / GRADIENT•	500ft (150m) ▲▲▲
•LEVEL OF DIFFICULTY•	🚶🚶 🚶🚶 🚶🚶
•PATHS•	Streets, well-built paths on tor; muddy path on Chalice Hill, 4 stiles
•LANDSCAPE•	Busy tourist town and small, steep hill
•SUGGESTED MAP•	aqua3 OS Explorer 141 Cheddar Gorge
•START / FINISH•	Grid reference: ST 498389
•DOG FRIENDLINESS•	Urban walk, with leads requested on tor
•PARKING•	Pay-and-display in Northload Street West
•PUBLIC TOILETS•	Northload car park and at Abbey entrance

Walk 30 Directions

From the **Market Cross** head down **Magdalene Street**, past the entrance to the **Glastonbury Abbey** grounds. On the right is St Margaret's Chapel, originally a 14th-century hospice for pilgrims.

We must leave aside the stories of King Arthur and Joseph of Arimathaea, enjoyable as they are, for we now know they were invented to raise visitor revenue for rebuilding works after the fire of 1184. This was a strategy which must surely qualify as the most persistent and effective advertising campaign of all time. Money was raised by the sale of indulgences (time-off-purgatory vouchers) and relics, and still flows into shops and offertory boxes today.

Beyond the chapel is the 18th-century **Pump Room**, indicating Glastonbury's brief period as a spa town. Cross a roundabout (with, on the right, the road to Street logically labelled 'Street Road' – it couldn't really have been 'Street Street'), keep ahead into **Fishers Hill**, then turn left into **Bere Lane**. Follow this to its end, passing the Rural Life Museum – this started life as a grange barn of Glastonbury Abbey.

At **Chilkwell Street** turn right on to a raised pavement. After ¼ mile (400m) you reach the Chalice Well and Gardens: its sinister blood-red waters once supplied the Abbey, and later the Pump House. It has been developed as a 'visitor attraction'

WHERE TO EAT AND DRINK

A wide selection of cafés and inns, the most striking being the **George and Pilgrim** hotel, which was built in the 14th century to accommodate overflow from the abbey's own hostelry. At the Market Cross the **King William** has a beer garden, real ales and food.

(with an entry fee). Turn left into **Well House Lane** and at once right, up a steep lane that leads on to **Glastonbury Tor**. The hill is made of layers of clay and blue limestone, with a cap of sandstone. Once the resistant sandstone has eroded away the tor will quickly collapse – but a geological age or two must pass before this happens. A dense cloud of legend and mystery hangs over Glastonbury Tor. This was a sacred site for the pagans, and then for over 1,000 years the Christian heart of the West Country.

WHAT TO LOOK FOR ⓘ

Medieval timber-frame cottages get resurfaced again and again through the centuries. Signs to look for are: steep roofs that were formerly thatch; low doorways; small windows; and very thick walls (shown at the window-openings). Examples at the walk start are No 1 and No 2 Market Place.

A concrete path with steps leads upwards. Kestrels hover in the updraft of the steep sides. At the top is the tower of a medieval chapel: this has been a sacred site since the 6th century, with an earlier chapel having collapsed in an earthquake. Richard Whiting, the last Abbot of Glastonbury, was hanged, drawn and quartered here for resisting the dissolution of the monasteries under Henry VIII. His dismembered parts were then displayed in nearby towns.

Turn right, in the direction of a reservoir far below, to find a concrete path that spirals down to the left. At the hill foot it turns right to a kissing gate. Cross a field to a gate on to a lane with a small car park. Turn left along the lane and bear left at a junction. After 140yds (128m) a stile on the right leads

---

WHILE YOU'RE THERE ⓘ

Visit **Glastonbury Abbey**. Among these hallowed ruins it's hard not to believe the legend that Joseph of Arimathaea brought the child Jesus to England, and built here a simple church of woven willow branches. Even without Arthur of Avalon, we still have an important abbey site with genuine Celtic roots; a showcase of the best of late medieval and Tudor architecture, and a hill with some of the best views in the county.

---

into a field. Bear left to a stile in the field corner. The hedged path beyond gets muddy in winter. Keep ahead down a tarred lane and, where this bends left, take the path ahead. It passes down **Chalice Hill** with a hedge on its left, to a lane below. At the foot of the lane the arched entrance of **Abbey House** is ahead. Turn right in **Lambrook Street**. On a wall on the left is a handsome Victorian fire-plate, indicating the nearby water supply, and at the junction of **High Street** is an old fountain.

Turn left to pass all the way along **High Street**. Almost every building here is noteworthy. St John's churchyard has a Glastonbury thorn – a cutting from the original miraculous thorn that grew from the staff of Joseph of Arimathaea. The thorn is supposed to flower twice, at Christmas and Easter.

On the left, a Victorian shopfront (for Feng Shui Crystals) stands beside the arch of the former White Horse Inn: here some of the losers were hanged after the Monmouth Rebellion of 1685. The Lake Village Museum is housed behind a Tudor façade of around 1500. At the end of **High Street** is the Market Cross, with the King William pub standing invitingly behind it.

...ore Borders at Three County Corner

An expedition through parts of Somerset, Dorset and Wiltshire, to Stourhead and Alfred's Tower.

•DISTANCE•	8½ miles (13.7km)
•MINIMUM TIME•	4hrs
•ASCENT / GRADIENT•	950ft (290m) ▲▲▲
•LEVEL OF DIFFICULTY•	👫 👫 👫
•PATHS•	Some tracks and some small paths and field edges, 7 stiles
•LANDSCAPE•	Tree-covered ridge
•SUGGESTED MAP•	aqua3 OS Explorer 142 Shepton Mallet
•START / FINISH•	Grid reference: ST 755314
•DOG FRIENDLINESS•	Moderate freedom on tracks and in woodland
•PARKING•	Penselwood church; some verge parking at Bleak Farm
•PUBLIC TOILETS•	Near Spread Eagle Inn – from Point ⑤ continue through arch for ½ mile (800m)

BACKGROUND TO THE WALK

Patriotic English people tend to think of Arthur and of Alfred, almost interchangeably, as the first king of their land; this is odd, as they were mortal enemies. Arthur, if he existed, ruled the Britons: a small, dark, Celtic people who spoke what we now call Old Welsh. Alfred spoke Old English, and belonged to the Saxon invaders. Eventually the invaders were themselves attacked by the Vikings and so started to think of themselves as the home side. Arthur's kingdom was Logres – which may or may not have been somewhere hereabouts.

Alfred, King of Somerset

Alfred was King of Somerset and, beyond that, King of Wessex; England had yet to be invented. Somerset, however, was a civilisation worth fighting for. Alfred fortified Burrow Mump (► Walk 36) as a strongpoint against the Danes, whose longships came at him up the River Parrett.

Defeated, he took refuge in the swamps of the 'Sumer Saete'. It was on the marsh island of Muchelney, south of Langport, that the demoralised and preoccupied King took shelter in the winter of AD 878 in a swine-herd's mud hut. The peasant's wife set him to watch the cakes, with disastrous results for the cookery but an eventual good outcome for Wessex... Emerging from his fen island, Alfred gathered the Saxons at Egbert's Stone, probably at the present-day site of Alfred's Tower. He defeated the Danes at Edington, now in Wiltshire.

Alfred's Reign

Alfred reigned from AD 873 to 888. He set up burhs, fortified towns, at Axbridge, Bath (where he reused the Roman defences), Langport and Watchet. His palace was at Cheddar. Alfred was a wise king who mixed thoughtfulness with ruthlessness, and realised that government based partly on consent was easier and worked better than government by force. His laws were put to a (non-elected) parliament of his witan: churchmen, nobles and local leaders.

Walk 31

Alfred's Tower

The tower we visit on this walk was placed in romantic commemoration of King Alfred; but its real point is as a place to turn round at the top of a scenic carriage drive from Stourhead – the turning circle for the carriages is still visible in the grass.

Today, while we decorate the hills with various money-making structures such as phone masts and television transmitters, to build a tower simply for decorative effect would as likely as not be dismissed instantly as a wicked intrusion on the landscape. Mind you, if we did build them, would they ever look so right in their surroundings as this tower, or the ruins on Glastonbury Tor and Burrow Mump (► Walk 36), or the monuments at Curry Rivel (► Walk 20) or Windmill Hill (► Walk 28)? Somehow our modern creations lack the air of permanence and sympathy with the landscape of these earlier construcions. There is a small charge if you want to go up the tower, but if its a clear day, it's the only way to get above the treetops for the total, three-county view.

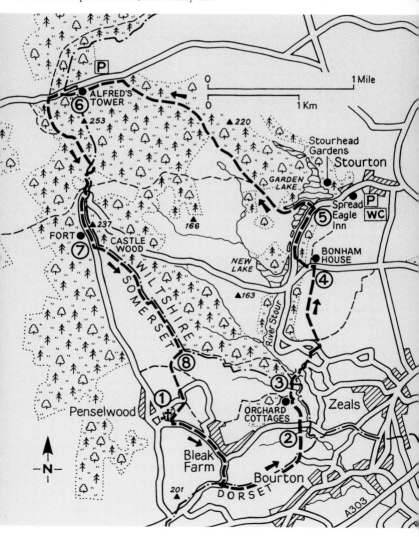

Walk 31

Walk 31 Directions

① Go through the churchyard to join a road beyond. Turn left through **Bleak Farm** village, then left into an inconspicuous sunken track. This ends at the top of a tarred lane; here turn left through a white gate, signed '**Pen Mill Hill**'. Head down to a kissing gate in a dip and follow a green track past a pond to a road.

> **WHILE YOU'RE THERE** ⓘ
> Visit the National Trust's **Stourhead House**. The lakes and ornamental buildings are glimpsed on the way past on the walk: for a fuller view you'll have to pay, but it's worth it for the vistas of ornamental water and silly little temples.

② Cross into a path waymarked '**Coombe Street**'. Pass below **Orchard Cottages**, then turn left over two stiles. Cross a stream in a dip to a stile below a thatched cottage. A woodland path bends to the right to a footbridge over the tiny **River Stour**.

③ From here to Point ④ is marked '**Stour Valley Way**'. Go up into a tarred lane and turn left. Keep ahead into a hedged way for 30yds (27m) to a stile. Go up and round left to another stile. The lane beyond leads up to a T-junction; go straight across and turn left into a bridleway track. Go through a gate

> **WHAT TO LOOK FOR** ⓘ
> **Buzzards** and **ravens** nest in Great Combe Woods. As there are no eagles in Somerset, any bird soaring high above the hill will be a buzzard. The raven is a large crow, with a deep croak and a slightly pointed (rather than fan-shaped) tail. Both birds are basically scavengers, with a taste for road-killed rabbit.

to follow the left edge of a field into a hedged track. This emerges opposite **Bonham House**.

④ Turn left, and at the second signpost bear right to a road below. Follow this to the right, to a rustic rock arch. A track on the left is signposted '**Alfred's Tower**'.

⑤ The track bends right and heads into a wooded valley with **Alfred's Tower** visible ahead. Finally it reaches open ground at the hilltop, with a road ahead. Turn left, in a grassy avenue, to Alfred's Tower.

⑥ Join the road ahead for 220yds (201m), down to a sunken path on the left signed '**Penselwood**'. Follow this, ignoring paths on both sides, on to a track descending to a major junction. Here bear right to a lane. Bear right again, on a road signed 'Penselwood'. This leads over a hilltop containing a hill fort. Descend for 100yds (91m) until open ground appears on the left.

> **WHERE TO EAT AND DRINK** ⓘ
> The **Spread Eagle Inn** is at the entrance to Stourhead House. To get there from Point ⑤ keep ahead through the rock arch for ½ mile (800m).

⑦ Cross a stile to head downhill with **Castle Wood** on your left, and blocks of young trees on your right. Move into the wood to join a track along its edge. At the corner of the wood, a waymarked gate on the right leads into fields.

⑧ Follow the left edge of the first field to two gates on the left, then keep ahead to a gate and a second gate beyond it. A track leads out to a road. Turn right to a sharp right-hand bend, where a gate starts a field path to **Penselwood church**.

Bruton Combes

A walk around and above beautiful Bruton, a typical Somerset town, built in the early wealth of the wool industry.

•DISTANCE•	4½ miles (7.2km)
•MINIMUM TIME•	2hrs 15min
•ASCENT / GRADIENT•	500ft (150m) ▲▲▲
•LEVEL OF DIFFICULTY•	🚶🚶 🚶🚶 🚶🚶
•PATHS•	Enclosed tracks, open fields, an especially muddy farmyard
•LANDSCAPE•	Steep, grassy hills and combes
•SUGGESTED MAP•	aqua3 OS Explorer 142 Shepton Mallet
•START / FINISH•	Grid reference: ST 684348
•DOG FRIENDLINESS•	On leads or under close control
•PARKING•	Free parking off Silver Street, 50yds (46m) west of church; larger car park in Upper Backway
•PUBLIC TOILETS•	Near Church Bridge (walk start) and signposted from there

BACKGROUND TO THE WALK

Bruton is a typical Somerset town: originally Saxon but made prosperous by monks in the Middle Ages. The Augustinians moved in around 1150 and soon upgraded from priory to abbey. In the 10th century Bruton was the county's seventh largest town – though this was achieved with a tax-paying population of just 85!

Woolly Thinking

In the Middle Ages England was a one-product economy. The basic unit of wealth was the 346lb (160kg) woolsack. In 1310 some 35,000 of these were exported; in 1421, 75 per cent of all customs duties were paid on wool. In Parliament at London, the Lord Chancellor sat on a woolsack as a constant reminder of where his government's money came from. (Today it has been replaced by a wool-stuffed chair.)

As the price of raw wool started to fall, England turned to the manufacture of cloth, adding value to the product before it left the country. Bruton was ahead of the game here. Back in 1240 the town built its first fulling mill, sited on Quaperlake Street. Here the cloth was washed with fullers' earth, a form of clay that acts as a natural de-greasing compound. (Fuller's earth absorbs water as well as grease; it is responsible for the peculiarly sticky mud encountered on the climb out of Combe Hay on Walk 48.) The washed wool was then felted with water-powered hammers.

The raw wool market had been dominated by trading barons, who frequently became real aristocratic barons as a result. But the cloth trade saw, and to a great extent caused, the rise of the English middle class of clothiers and merchants. Their wool wealth rebuilt the church and a century later added its unusual second tower; they built the High Street and endowed the almshouses. Bruton clothiers traded with merchants in Hampshire, Dorset and London, and exported through the ports of Dorset. In the 1540s Bruton's fullers were importing woad (for dyeing) from the far Azores by way of Bristol. The Abbey saw its interests as parallel with those of the town, and subsidised the market cross and the licensing of fairs.

Walk 32

Wool Unspun

Mechanisation of the spinning and weaving processes was getting under way in the 1820s, but depression set in during the 1830s and Somerset never caught up with Lancashire. Hence Somerset wool villages remain non-industrial and pretty. Many medieval buildings survive behind the (fairly) modern shop signs and under the paintwork. Where others have collapsed through the ages, replacements have been inserted in the style of every century but always with sympathy. Today, competition from synthetic materials means the price of a fleece barely pays the wages of the man who shears it. In Bruton you'll see the evidence of wool wealth on every side. The one thing you probably won't see is a sheep.

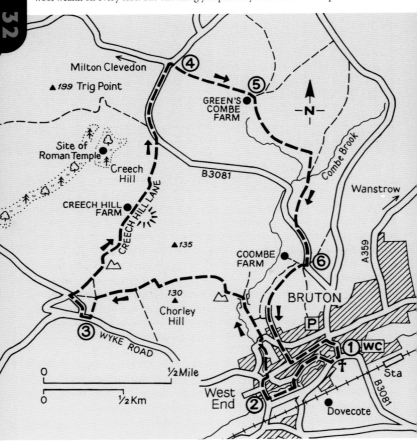

Walk 32 Directions

① With the church on your left and the bridge on your right, head down **Silver Street** for 30yds (27m) to a small car park in **Coombe Street**. The old packhorse bridge over the **River Brue** leads into

Lower Backway. Turn left for 350yds (320m), ignoring an arch leading towards a footbridge but then taking a path between railed fences to a second footbridge. Turn right along the river to **West End**.

② Turn right over the river and right again into the end of **High**

Street, but at once turn off uphill on to a walled path called **Mill Dam**. At the lane above turn right along a track signed 'Huish Lane'. Just after a footbridge fork left: the hedged track is fairly steep and muddy, bending right then left to a lane (**Wyke Road**).

③ Turn right for a few steps, then right again, and after 220yds (201m) turn right past farm buildings on to an uphill track, **Creech Hill Lane**. This becomes a hedged tunnel, then emerges at **Creech Hill Farm**. This may be one of the county's less tidy farms, but boasts one of its finest views. Pass along the front of the farm and out to the **B3081**. Turn left over the hill crest to a triangular junction.

④ Turn right for 40yds (37m) to a public bridleway sign and a gate on the right. Go straight down the combe below; at its foot keep to the left of **Green's Combe Farm** and above an intermittent wall, to turn down through a gate between the farm buildings.

> **WHAT TO LOOK FOR** ⓘ
> Bartons – narrow medieval streets, some no more than enclosed passageways – lead down off the High Street towards Lower Backway. The word 'barton' actually means a farmyard. These passages were originally places for keeping the household livestock at a time when urban sophistication meant not having the cow living in the house.

> **WHERE TO EAT AND DRINK** ⓘ
> The **Castle Inn** (pizzas) and the slightly more upmarket **Sun Inn** are both ancient establishments in the High Street. The **Montague** at Shepton Montague has never installed the usual bar plumbing; the beer still comes straight out of a barrel supported on a cradle. It serves good bar and restaurant food and children and dogs are welcome.

⑤ Continue down the farm's access track for ¼ mile (400m) until it bends right. Here keep ahead through a field gate with a blue waymarker, on to a green track. After 200yds (183m), beside three stumps, turn downhill, to the left of a row of hazels, to a gate. Pass through a small wood to a gate and waymarked track. When this emerges into open field follow the fence above to join the **B3081**. Turn left, uphill, to the entrance to **Coombe Farm**.

⑥ Ignoring a stile on the left, go through an ivy-covered wall gap, then down the driveway for barely a dozen paces before turning left on to a wide path under sycamore trees. The path rises gently, with a bank on its left. On reaching open grassland, keep to the left edge to find a descending path that becomes **St Catherine's Lane**. Weavers' cottages are on the right as the street descends steeply into **Bruton**. Turn left along the **High Street**. At its end turn right down **Patwell Street** to **Church Bridge**.

> **WHILE YOU'RE THERE** ⓘ
> The working water mill at **Gant's Mill** dates back to 1290, reflecting Bruton's early prosperity. Its uses through the centuries reflect the business of Somerset. Originally it was a fulling mill (► Background to the Walk); when wool declined, it was adapted to power spinning machinery for the short-lived silk industry. For the last hundred years it has been grinding barley and corn for cattle feeds. Today the main product processed here is the tourist! The working mill is surrounded by a water garden. Opening times are restricted so check with the tourist information office at Bruton or Yeovil.

Nunney and its Village, Castle and Combe

Visiting a stone-built village with a moated castle, once besieged in the Civil War, on this wander through woodland and pasture.

•DISTANCE•	3 miles (4.8km)
•MINIMUM TIME•	1hr 15min
•ASCENT / GRADIENT•	100ft (30m) ▲ ▲ ▲
•LEVEL OF DIFFICULTY•	🚶 🚶 🚶
•PATHS•	Broad, riverside path, pasture, then leafy track, 8 stiles
•LANDSCAPE•	Deeply wooded stream valley, breaking out into open pasture with wide views
•SUGGESTED MAP•	aqua3 OS Explorer 142 Shepton Mallet
•START / FINISH•	Grid reference: ST 736456
•DOG FRIENDLINESS•	Well-behaved dogs can run free in Nunney Combe and on final track
•PARKING•	Short-stay parking at Nunney Market Square; small lay-by at end of a public footpath 150yds (137m) up Castle Hill
•PUBLIC TOILETS•	None on route

BACKGROUND TO THE WALK

The castle at Nunney is awkward to spot, huddled down among the houses, but once found it will not be forgotten. Built in 1373 by Sir John de la Mare, it's a superb structure with large corner towers and a proper moat all the way round. Sir John had fought with the Black Prince in France, and his gatehouse here included some of the very latest French fashions in construction. Through its ruined walls we catch glimpses of the swans and ducks in the moat and the rose-hung cottages of the village.

Costume Drama

The nearby village church, which is attractive in its own right, has interesting effigies of the De la Mere family over two centuries. Such effigies are of particular interest to costume designers, who otherwise would have no idea of what Elizabethan outfits looked like from the back. This is important when you're making a film such as *Shakespeare in Love* – Gwyneth Paltrow can't always be facing the camera! Also worth a look is the font cover from 1684, which is an ornate cone of carved wood.

Uncivil War

Although particular towns had particular loyalties during the Civil War (Wells for Royalist, Taunton for Parliamentarian), Somerset as a whole was not carried away into warfare. Indeed, a local, low-technology force of 'Clubmen' (the first bouncers?) was formed to discourage either side from entering the county. Armies brought inconvenience: 'such uncivil drinkers and thirsty souls that a barrel of good beer trembles at the sight of them, and the whole house nothing but a rendezvous of tobacco and spitting' wrote a Tolland farmer obliged to play host to the Parliamentarians in 1647. Still, Britain's civil wars must be considered civilised when compared with the Thirty Years' War which ravaged Germany around the same time, where the resulting famine and plague reduced the population of the countryside by a third.

Taunton was besieged twice, and Bridgwater once. Somerset saw one battle, at Langport. Part of the Royalist army under Lord Goring had arrived too late to get defeated at the Battle of Naseby: Fairfax and the New Model Army caught up with them at the fords of the Wagg Rhyne and defeated them there instead. After the battle, Colonel Prater, its owner, took refuge in Nunney Castle with eight Irishmen. The villagers must have been alarmed at the prospect of a siege taking place right among their houses. In the event the castle fell without much of a fight, although one cannonball lodged in the wall of the nearby church. Afterwards the Roundheads deliberately ruined the castle to prevent its being reoccupied. Somerset's sufferings were to come 40 years later, in the Monmouth Rebellion.

Walk 33

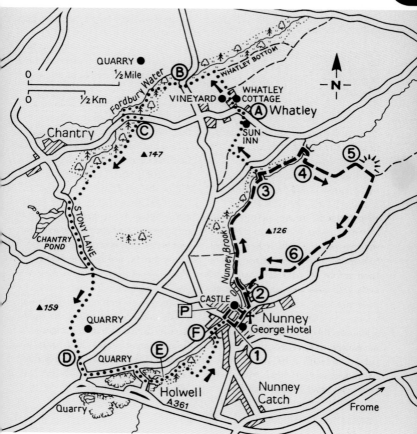

Walk 33 Directions

① From Nunney's **Market Square** cross the brook and at once turn right to **Nunney Castle** (entry is free). Having inspected the castle, return and pass to the right, across a footbridge, to the church. Some 80yds (73m) further on, where the street starts uphill, turn left into **Donkey Lane**.

Walk 33

② Follow the lane past a high wall on the left, to a gate with a signpost. Keep ahead, leaving the track after 150yds (137m) for a small gate ahead into woods. A wide path leads downstream with the **Nunney Brook** on its left. After about ¾ mile (1.2km) a track runs across the valley.

> ### WHAT TO LOOK FOR ⓘ
> Less than a century after the Civil War, Nunney had shrugged off its thrilling military history to become a prosperous village of clothiers and weavers. Look out for **weavers' cottages** with large windows to light the looms. Opposite the church is a riverside ramp: in the 18th century woollen cloth was washed and stretched here.

③ Turn left, as a signpost suggests, to cross the brook; immediately turn right over a broken stile. Continue along the stream on a nettly, often muddy path. After 350yds (320m) the path climbs away from the stream to join a track above. Turn right on this, to cross the stream on a high-arched bridge. The track bends right, through a gate: before the next gate look out for an old grey gate on the left with a waymarking arrow.

④ Go up the right-hand side of a narrow field to a field gate (no stile). Continue uphill on the left-hand edge for just 50yds (46m), to a stile in the hedge. This stile, like

> ### WHERE TO EAT AND DRINK ⓘ
> The fairly smart **George Hotel** at Nunney has a restaurant and a beer garden (and also a poltergeist). It welcomes children but not dogs. The restaurant menu includes fresh fish from Padstow daily. The garden is believed to have been used for judicial executions and a ghostly woman has been heard wailing.

> ### WHILE YOU'RE THERE ⓘ
> Somerset has the stony soils of the best French wine-growing areas – but not, alas, the French sunshine. **Whatley Vineyard and Herb Garden** is near Nunney and on the route of Walk 34. You can wander round the vineyard and the walled herb garden. Wine-tastings are offered for large groups only.

those that follow, has a waymarker giving the direction across the next field. Turn half-right as the arrow indicates, to slant up to a hedge and follow it along the top of the field to a stile at the corner. As this is the crest of a broad ridge, there are now views ahead to the hills in the west.

⑤ Turn left around the field to a stile in the next corner. Once over this, turn half-right and go straight across the field to a visble stile at its furthest corner – this turns out to be a double stile. Once across, follow the left-hand edge of the long field ahead. At its corner cross a stile between two gateways and turn right. After 400yds (366m), and before the end of the field, watch out for a stile on the right.

⑥ This leads into a narrow track between over-arching hedges. It bends to the left and then the right, then descends to become a street leading into Nunney. This runs down to join **Donkey Lane** on the outward route, with the church just 300yds (274m) ahead.

Two Bottoms from Nunn

A longer, more strenuous and slightly brambly ramble.
See map and information panel for Walk 33

•DISTANCE•	5¼ miles (8.4km)
•MINIMUM TIME•	2hrs 45min
•ASCENT / GRADIENT•	750ft (230m) ▲▲▲
•LEVEL OF DIFFICULTY•	👥 👥 👥

Walk 34 Directions
(Walk 33 option)

From Point ③ cross **Nunney Brook** and head up to a road. Cross to a stile and go up to a kissing gate on the right. Slant gently uphill, eventually reaching the Sun Inn, Point Ⓐ. Turn left to the entrance to **Whatley Vineyard**, and follow waymarkers on to a driveway towards **Whatley Cottage**. Keep to its left to a gap, and then to the right of a house called **Fortywinks**. Head straight down, over two stiles in new fencing, to the top of the steep wood of **Whatley Bottom**. Turn left to the next corner, where a stile leads down to a lane, Point Ⓑ.

The path continues opposite, along the top of steep wood. Beyond, a large quarry is removing this part of the landscape. After 200yds (183m) the path slants down past two ancient yew trees to **Fordbury Water**.

Follow this upstream through woods to a stile. Don't cross, but slant up left to a road. Turn uphill for 220yds (201m) to a footpath signpost, Point Ⓒ. Cross and follow the top edge of the wood on faint paths (the good path at the foot of the wood is not a right of way). A barbed-wire fence marks a path-line descending to reach **Stony Lane**.

Turn left for ½ mile (800m) to a road junction. Directly opposite is a green lane between high banks. This passes beside another quarry to reach a busy road, Point Ⓓ. Turn right for 150yds (137m) to a junction. Follow a minor road on the left ('Nunney 1') above yet another quarry, which whitens the hedges with dust. At its end a tiny lane leads steeply downhill. A footpath sign points down to the stream, with a footbridge a few steps away on the left. Turn left, downstream, to pass through an oolitic breeze block depot into a final streamside wood, Point Ⓔ.

After 220yds (201m) the path passes below a small crag and turns uphill to a stile. Continue ahead, at first with the wood on the left, then across open field to a cattle trough. Turn left towards the tower of **Nunney church**, joining the wood edge on the left. Continue along the field edge above the woodland. At a wall corner steps lead down to a footbridge, Point Ⓕ. A walled path leads between gardens into **Nunney**. Turn right, passing a prison for very small miscreants, to the village centre.

Along the Fosse Way to Shepton Mallet

Catch a bus for this linear stroll along a Roman motorway.

Walk 35

•DISTANCE•	3½ miles (5.7km)
•MINIMUM TIME•	1hr 40min
•ASCENT / GRADIENT•	300ft (90m) ▲▲ ▲
•LEVEL OF DIFFICULTY•	衸 衸衸 衸衸
•PATHS•	Firm, reasonably mud-free track, field paths, 2 stiles
•LANDSCAPE•	Gentle hills of eastern Mendips
•SUGGESTED MAP•	aqua3 OS Explorer 142 Shepton Mallet
•START•	Grid reference: ST 635473
•FINISH•	Grid reference: ST 618436
•DOG FRIENDLINESS•	Well-behaved dogs can run off lead, except on road
•PARKING•	Main pay-and-display, Old Market Road, Shepton Mallet
•PUBLIC TOILETS•	Market Square, Shepton Mallet
•NOTE•	Buses leave from the Cenotaph, ¼ mile (400m) from main car park and 100yds (91m) from tourist information centre. Eight buses daily on six different services

Walk 35 Directions

The bus stops at the **Oakhill Inn**. The walk starts along **Fosse Road**, passing some 17th-century cottages to **Fosse Cottage** on the left. Here the track of the Fosse Way sets off on the right. The Fosse Way was the 4th-century equivalent of the M5 motorway, running from the south coast to Lincoln. Ilchester, at the junction with the road to the coast over the Polden Hills, became the local centre of government, with rich civil servants building villas in the countryside around. Shepton Mallet was a Roman industrial town beside the road, and Bath, with its hot springs, can be considered as an early motorway service station.

At the first rise the track becomes a sunken path, which over the years has eroded down so deeply into the

ground that the track abandons it for a dog-leg out to the right. It rejoins the Roman line 300yds (274m) further on. Views on the left are across the eastern Mendips. The track runs up to a minor road at the top of the slope.

The direct route through the Woodland Trust's wood ahead will involve a steep descent. Those wishing to avoid this can turn right, along the road, for 70yds (64m) to where the signposted 'Fosse Way' continues on the opposite side. The slightly more adventurous can cross directly into the wood, to follow a small path ahead. This drops steeply to the corner of open ground and continues along the wood edge to rejoin the main track.

Roman roads stayed in use for centuries after the Romans' departure; with new roads being

Walk 35

WHILE YOU'RE THERE
Steam trains of the **East Somerset Railway** run for 2½ miles (4km) along the 'Strawberry Line'. The 1 in 56 (1.8%) gradient is claimed as the steepest restored railway in Britain. 'Oil the Engine and Drive the Train' courses are offered.

built on the foundations of the old, the Fosse Way here became, through the ages, the A37. Elsewhere it was a useful landmark to define the boundary of a medieval estate: today that line may be a field edge, and possibly a parish boundary as well. On Beacon Hill the otherwise invisible line of the old road is marked by parish boundary stones. In just one or two places the old road has remained in use for farm and foot traffic; our walk follows one such stretch.

Once out of the wood the fenced track continues ahead. Without a map, a straight line is the easiest to survey and lay out on the ground. Often the road is lined up on a convenient sighting point; here, the barrows on Beacon Hill seem to have been the place the Romans aimed for. Modern-day mystics claim the barrows mark the intersection of energy-paths called leys that fly like arrows all over the countryside. The sensitive Celts laid their paths along such lines and the Romans simply built theirs on top.

On reaching a lane, turn left for 150yds (137m), then back right for 250yds (229m). The **Fosse Way** track continues on the left, just past a stagnant pond. The track rises gradually, then starts to descend with Shepton Mallet in sight ahead. As the descent steepens, bare rock shows in the bed of the trackway. Ignore a barred stile on the right, and continue past a concrete shed

(also on the right) to a fenced gas-board hut. After another 200yds (183m) comes a stile on the right, with a viaduct ahead.

Cross a field towards the viaduct, passing to the right of two free-standing ash trees, then bearing left towards a conspicuous stile. A path leads on under the viaduct and into the end of a street. Where this street bends left keep ahead into a walled path, with glimpses into the **Jubilee Gardens** on the right. Emerge into a small car park.

WHAT TO LOOK FOR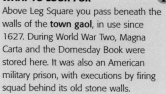
Above Leg Square you pass beneath the walls of the **town gaol**, in use since 1627. During World War Two, Magna Carta and the Domesday Book were stored here. It was also an American military prison, with executions by firing squad behind its old stone walls.

Turn right past a Georgian brewery and 20th-century cider works; go under an overhead pipe and turn left at a 'Babycham' plastic chamois(!). Weavers' cottages are on the right as **Garston Street** leads into **Leg Square**. Turn left into a short cul-de-sac, and at **Hill Cottage** turn right into a walled path, with **Gaol Lane** continuing uphill above. Turn right on a paved path ('No Bikes') with a filled-in archway on the left, to pass the church and reach the market place. From the **Market Cross** head up the **High Street**: turn right at the first set of traffic lights for the main car park, or keep ahead for the tourist information centre.

WHERE TO EAT AND DRINK
The bus from Shepton Mallet passes the Oakhill Brewery. The beer must travel just 300yds (274m) to reach the **Oakhill Inn**, which is the walk's start point.

Catching the Burrow Mump on the Levels

A gentle wander around the Somerset Levels near Burrowbridge leading up to a hump called a 'mump'.

•DISTANCE•	5¼ miles (8.4km)
•MINIMUM TIME•	2hrs 15min
•ASCENT / GRADIENT•	150ft (50m)
•LEVEL OF DIFFICULTY•	🚶 🚶 🚶
•PATHS•	Tracks, paths, unfrequented field edges, 6 stiles
•LANDSCAPE•	Flat pasture with ditches and one surprising, small hill
•SUGGESTED MAP•	aqua3 OS Explorer 140 Quantock Hills & Bridgwater
•START / FINISH•	Grid reference: ST 360395
•DOG FRIENDLINESS•	Good on drove tracks where dogs separated from livestock by deep ditches
•PARKING•	National Trust car park (free) at Burrow Mump
•PUBLIC TOILETS•	None on route

BACKGROUND TO THE WALK

After the last Ice Age, around 10–18,000 years ago, this ground was under the sea; in one sense it still is, as the high tide in the Bristol Channel rises up to 20ft (6m) above the fields and ditches. If the sea ever does get back in, it will lap against Glastonbury Tor and make Bridgwater and Burnham reminiscent (albeit in just one sense) of Venice – they will have canals instead of streets.

The draining of this ground started in Roman times, but gathered pace in the early Middle Ages. The three centuries following the Norman conquest (until the Black Death) brought increasing prosperity and security, shown by, among other things, the windmills that sprung up along the Polden Hills. The growing population required more land to be drained for the plough and the cow.

Summer Pasture

The water-meadows around Barrow Mump were first drained by the monks of Glastonbury Abbey in about 1255. They raised walls to keep out the pervasive waters of the River Parrett, to form fertile water-meadows. In winter these would be allowed to flood, their soils enriched by silt from the river. In summer the drained grasslands formed highly fertile grazing land for their cattle, with convenient and effective wet fencing and plenty of fresh drinking water. This agricultural process may give us the origin of 'Sumor Saete' or Somerset, the 'land of summer'.

Drainage was continued through the ages: the King's Sedgemoor Drain, with its complex arrangement of sluices and pumps, was constructed in the 19th century; and managed drainage came to the Huntspill River area during World War Two. Wind pumps were replaced by steam-powered engines and then by the diesel one that may be heard thumping in the distance at the start of the walk. Our route is around the drove tracks and the river barriers, with a final ascent of Burrow Mump for an overall view.

Obvious Strongpoint

In the days when the surrounding ground was swamp, Burrow Mump was occupied by the local Celtic people against the Romans. In the Anglo-Saxon era, it was a strongpoint of King Alfred's; he fortified it against Danish raiders coming up the River Parrett. Later it held a Norman castle. Once the surroundings were drained its tactical value decreased, and the present Chapel of St Michael was built by the monks of Athelney Abbey. Even so it remained an obvious strongpoint, and the chapel was held by the Royalists in 1645 after their crushing defeat by Cromwell's New Model Army at the Battle of Langport. It was partially destroyed on that occasion, restored in the 18th century, and has fallen back down again since then.

View from a Hill

The summit, though only raised 100ft (30m) above the sea-level surroundings, commands a wide and interesting view. Half a dozen parish churches can be seen in various directions. The closest of these, looking due north from the Mump, is St Mary's in Westonzoyland, with its square tower. Here captured rebels were imprisoned by government troops after their defeat at the Battle of Sedgemoor in 1685. Closer at hand, the distinctive pattern of droves (tracks) and walls (river barriers, originally 12ft (4m) high and 30ft (10m) wide) can be seen around the water-meadows.

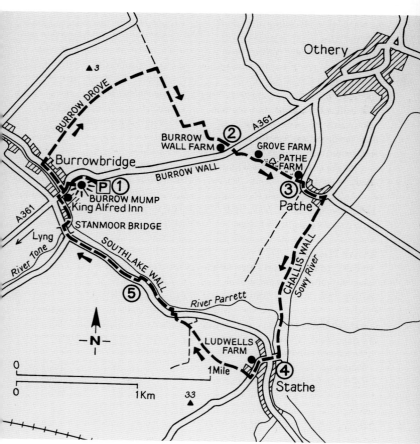

Walk 36

Walk 36 Directions

① A gate leads on to the base of the **Mump**. Keep round to the right to a small gate and steps down to the **Burrow Bridge**. Just before the bridge turn right into **Riverside**. After 350yds (320m) turn right into **Burrow Drove**, which becomes a tractor track. On either side and between the fields are deep ditches, coated in bright green pondweed. At a T-junction there's a culvert of 19th-century brick on the left. Here turn right on a new track: it passes behind **Burrow Wall Farm**, to meet the busy **A361**.

② A 'public footpath' sign points to a track opposite. After just 30yds (27m) turn left over a stile. With the bushy **Burrow Wall** on your right, cross a field to the usually very muddy **Grove Farm**. Go through two gates to continue along fields beside woodland on the left. At the end of the second field an awkward rusty gate leads up between brambles to a green track: turn right here to reach a lane near **Pathe Farm**.

③ Turn right along the lane, ignoring a track on the right, to reach a side-lane on the right. Here cross a bridge to a hedge-gap on the right and a very narrow footbridge. Continue through several fields, with a wide rhyne (or ditch) on the

right. Near by, on the left, is the low banking of **Challis Wall**, concealing the Sowy River. The ditch on the right gradually gets smaller. When it finally ends bear right to the **River Parrett** and follow it to a latticework road bridge. Cross this into the edge of **Stathe**.

> **WHERE TO EAT AND DRINK** ⓘ
> The **King Alfred Inn** at Burrowbridge offers food as well as beer. Like many traditional Somerset inns, it also has a skittle alley.

④ Keep ahead through the village, past a phone box and **Ludwells Farm**, to a stile on the right waymarked '**Macmillan Way**'. Follow the right edge of one field to a gate; cross to the hedge opposite and follow it round to the left, to a stile. Continue with a hedge on your right to a gate, where a hedged track leads to a road. Turn left, perhaps scrambling up the banking, to walk on the **Southlake Wall** between road and river.

⑤ As the road turns away from the river, rejoin it. Once across **Stanmoor Bridge** a waymarker points to the right for a riverbank path to **Burrowbridge**. Turn right and, this time, climb to the top of **Burrow Mump** for an overview of the entire walk and much of Somerset as well.

> **WHILE YOU'RE THERE** ⓘ
> A short distance down the Parrett is the **Westonzoyland Pumping Station Museum**. It has two centuries' worth of machinery, and on some Sundays you can see a steam-powered pump of 1861 actually at work – check with the Bridgwater tourist information centre for dates and times.

> **WHAT TO LOOK FOR** ⓘ
> **Pollard willow**: on the banks of the drove grow willow trees like an infant's drawing – a bare trunk, topped by a sudden round bush. Historically, these trees have been chopped back, or pollarded, every ten years. The poles were for firewood, or for a dozen uses around the farm. Today, willow timber is the best raw material for making corrugated cardboard.

Westhay Peatland Reserve

A nature ramble through reconstructed peat marshland, including a brief walk on water.

•DISTANCE•	4¾ miles (7.7km)
•MINIMUM TIME•	2hrs 15min
•ASCENT / GRADIENT•	250ft (80m) ▲▲▲
•LEVEL OF DIFFICULTY•	🚶🚶 🚶🚶 🚶🚶
•PATHS•	Mostly smooth, level paths and tracks, 2 stiles
•LANDSCAPE•	Reed beds and water-meadows
•SUGGESTED MAP•	aqua3 OS Explorer 141 Cheddar Gorge
•START / FINISH•	Grid reference: ST 456437
•DOG FRIENDLINESS•	On leads in reserve, can be free on drove tracks
•PARKING•	Free car park at Decoy Pool, signposted from public road
•PUBLIC TOILETS•	None on route
•NOTE•	To bypass rough part, follow lane between Points ④ and ⑥

BACKGROUND TO THE WALK

At Westhay Moor the Somerset Trust for Nature Conservation (STNC) is carefully recreating the original peat wetland from a time before drainage and peat cuttings. This involves raising the water table with polythene barriers, and importing sphagnum moss and peatland plants from Cumbria. 'True blanket bog', one of their notices reminds us, 'should wobble when walked on...' And while these rehabilitated peat diggings are very good news for waterfowl and the nightjar, for rare spiders and the bog bush cricket, they are still a long way from the original Somerset moor.

Moor or Morass?

'Moor' is the same as 'mire' or 'morass'; the Saxon word first occurs in the account of King Alfred taking refuge at Muchelney. For the Saxons the moor was a place of mystery and fear. About 1,500 years ago the monster Grendel was the original 'Thing from the Swamp' in the poem of *Beowulf*. Open water alternated with reed beds and mud. The inhabitants moved around by boat, or by wading, or on stilts. Even if you could see out over the reeds it rarely helped as the mist would come down. And, at nightfall, the will o' the wisp misled you into the unstable mud, just in case you hadn't been swallowed up in it already.

If you did ever get out on to firm land, you were quite likely to be infected with ague or marsh fever. Even the modern name, 'malaria', reflects its supposed origin in the misty airs of the wetlands. Actually it was transmitted by mosquitoes that bred in the stagnant water. Oliver Cromwell, a fenman from East Anglia, died of malaria. It persisted in the marshes of Essex into the 20th century and may return with global warming in the 21st.

Wet Refuge

For those who knew its ways, the moor was the safest of refuges. Iron Age tribes built a village on wooden piles near Glastonbury; the Romans complained of the way the tribesmen would hide with only their heads above the water. Alfred found safety from the Danes here, as did the monks of Glastonbury.

Walk 37

Wealth in the Wet

The moor was also, in its own way, wealthy. The less wet sections grew a rich summer pasture, fertilised by the silt of the winter floods. It's no coincidence that Britain's most famous cheese comes from the edge of the Levels. The deep, moist soil also grew heavy crops of hemp. Henry VIII made the growing of this useful plant compulsory, as it supplied cordage and sailcloth for the navy. Today, under its Latin name of *Cannabis sativa*, it is, of course, strictly forbidden. The wetter ground yielded osiers for baskets and reed for thatch; wildfowl and fish; and goosefeather quills for penmen. Fuel was peat, or willow poles from the pollarded trees whose roots supported the ditches. And the rent for this desirable property was often paid in live eels.

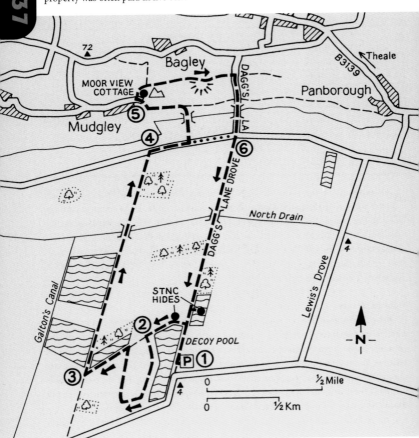

Walk 37 Directions

① Head into the reserve on a broad track, with **Decoy Pool** hiding behind reeds on the left. At the end of the lake a kissing gate leads to the STNC hide, with a broad path continuing between high reedbeds. Ignore a gate on the left ('No Visitor Access') but go through a kissing gate 60yds (55m) further on.

② A fenced track runs through peat ground, where birches are being felled to recreate blanket bog.

WHAT TO LOOK FOR
One rare bird of prey, the **hobby**, is worth looking out for on this walk. This small falcon is about the same size as a kestrel but looks a lot smaller because of its very fast and agile flight. It sometimes chases down small birds, but mostly it hunts dragonflies.

The track turns right; now take a kissing gate on the left for a path through trees. At its end a new track leads back through the peat. At the end turn left to reach a gate on to the next of the 'droves' or raised trackways through the peatland.

③ Turn right, passing hides and crossing a bridge over the wide **North Drain**; the land on each side now comprises water-meadows. The track leads to a lane.

④ If you wish to omit the field paths above (which are rough, but give a splendid view over the reserve), simply turn right, going along the road for 650yds (594m) to a junction, Point ⑥. Otherwise turn right as far as a right-hand bend, and continue for 175yds (160m) to where gates are on both sides of the road. Go through the left-hand one (with a red-painted marker) and cross to a gate and bridge over a ditch. Follow the left edge of the next field to its corner. Turn left through a gate and follow field edges to a small orchard. Turn right, up to the end of a tarred lane.

⑤ Turn left along the road to an uphill path to the left of **Moor View Cottage** – this becomes overgrown and quite steep – to a stile on the right. Cross the tops of five fields. In the sixth field drop slightly to pass below farm buildings (there is a helpful signpost here). A gate leads into a small orchard, with a

signposted gate on to **Dagg's Lane** just above. Turn down the lane to the road below.

⑥ Directly opposite Dagg's Lane is the track, **Dagg's Lane Drove**. This runs between meadows then re-enters the reserve, passing between pools left by peat extraction. Look out for a path on the left signposted to a hide. This leads out excitingly on stilts above the flooded mire. Return from the hide and rejoin the drove track, which quickly leads back to the car park.

WHERE TO EAT AND DRINK
The **Bird in Hand** is an old-style country inn at Westhay Bridge over the River Brue. Well-behaved dogs are welcome.

WHILE YOU'RE THERE
The **Peat Moors Centre** at Westhay has reconstructions of the Glastonbury Lake Village and of the oldest road in Britain, the Sweet Track – built in the Stone Age 6,000 years ago. It also has a newly-hacked Stone Age log boat.

Deep Romantic Ebbor

The small but sublime limestone gorge that inspired Coleridge.

•DISTANCE•	4¾ miles (7.7km)
•MINIMUM TIME•	2hrs 30min
•ASCENT / GRADIENT•	700ft (210m) ▲▲ ▲
•LEVEL OF DIFFICULTY•	🚶 🚶 🚶
•PATHS•	Small paths and field edges, with a rugged descent, 9 stiles
•LANDSCAPE•	Vast view across the Levels, then tight little gorge
•SUGGESTED MAP•	aqua3 OS Explorer 141 Cheddar Gorge
•START / FINISH•	Grid reference: ST 521484
•DOG FRIENDLINESS•	English Nature asks that dogs to be on leads in reserve
•PARKING•	Lane above Wookey Hole (optional, small fee)
•PUBLIC TOILETS•	At Wookey Hole's visitor car park

BACKGROUND TO THE WALK

In the introduction I made a facetious comparison between Somerset and Snowdonia. All the same, it's significant that when the poet Samual Taylor Coleridge (1772–1834) wanted to paint in words the ultimate in sublime landscape, he based his poem not on Snowdonia (which he had visited) but on Somerset. The setting of *Kubla Khan* (published in 1816) is based partly on Culbone Combe, on the Exmoor Coast, and partly on memories of a visit to Wookey Hole and Ebbor. So we have: 'the deep romantic chasm that slanted, down a green hill, athwart a cedern covert; a savage place!' While down at Wookey Hole (though you'll have to pay to see it): 'Alph, the sacred river ran, through caverns measureless to man…'.

To the writers and painters of the Romantic period, a landscape could be merely beautiful – or it could be sublime. A scene that's 'sublime' goes far beyond the merely pretty: it induces awe and even terror. It stills the noisy chattering mind, to the point of breaking through into the 'divine Reality' that lies behind the world. Today most of us don't believe in the divine Reality, and aren't driven to sort our views into categories and seek out the sublime. And yet I've felt it on Glastonbury Tor at sunset (▶ Walk 30) and I've found it at midnight on the Quantocks whilst staring down on some very 21st-century streetlights.

Ornamental Vision

It's interesting to compare *Kubla Khan* with Stourhead Garden (▶ Walk 31): the walls and towers are there; the incense-bearing trees; even the domed shapes of the buildings. Not that Stourhead's designer, Henry Hoare, was copying the poem, it's just that he and Coleridge were both after the same thing. There was a third category of satisfactory scenery: the picturesque. This is one that's arranged correctly, with foreground, middleground, and a hill wall shutting off the end. The foreground should have some ornamental peasants or brigands, from whom a carefully placed river or country lane leads the eye into the scene.

Turning from the sublime to the ridiculous, or at least the trivial: Coleridge did pronounce 'Kubla Khan' to rhyme with 'Measureless to man'. We know this from a letter of Dorothy Wordsworth's where she puns on 'Kubla Khan' and 'watering Khan'. Wordsworth himself mocked those of us who only go walking for the sake of the view – the 'craving for a prospect', as he called it. But Ebbor Gorge is impressive whatever its landscape category.

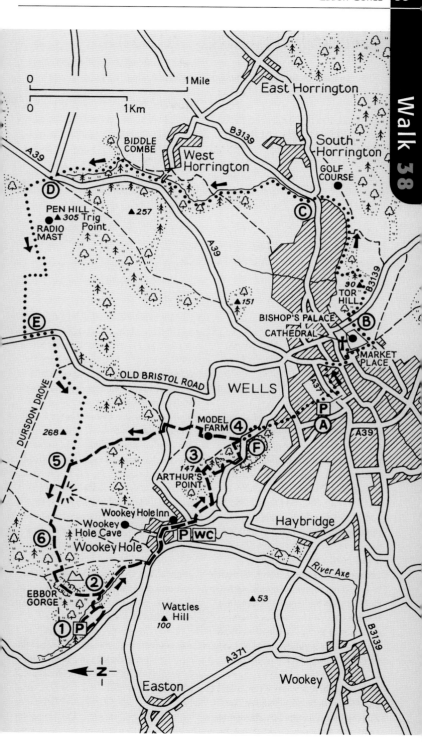

Walk 38 Directions

① From the noticeboard at the top end of the car park descend a stepped path. After a clearing, turn left (signposted '**The Gorge**'). The wide path crosses the stream to another junction.

② Turn right, away from the gorge, and follow the valley down to a road. Turn left, to pass through the village of **Wookey Hole**. At its end the road bends right; take a kissing gate on the left with a '**West Mendip Way**' waymarker post. After two more kissing gates turn left up a spur to a stile and the top of **Arthur's Point**.

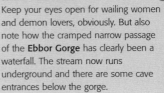

WHILE YOU'RE THERE
Wookey Hole Caves – the 'absolutely top hole' – was first recorded as a tourist attraction in 1480, when visitors had to bring their own rushlight tapers. The underground River Ax and the vast chambers are now dramatically illuminated by electric lighting.

③ Bear right for 60yds (55m) into woods again. Beware: hidden in the brambles ahead is the top of a quarry crag. So, turn right, down to a stile. Go down the field edge to a kissing gate, and bear left between boulders back into the wood. After a sharp little rise bear right, contouring to join **Lime Kiln Lane** below. This bends left with, again, a path on the left diverting through the bottom of the wood. This emerges at the end of a short field track, which is followed down to a footpath signpost.

④ Turn sharp left, on a track that passes through **Model Farm**, to **Tynings Lane**. Turn left for 85yds (78m) to a signposted stile on the

right. Go up with a fence on your right, then bear left to a gate with a stile. Go straight up the next, large field, aiming for a gateway with tractor ruts running into it. A track leads up through a wood and a field to a gate. Slant upwards in the same direction to another gate next to a stile 100yds (91m) below the field's top left corner.

WHAT TO LOOK FOR
Keep your eyes open for wailing women and demon lovers, obviously. But also note how the cramped narrow passage of the **Ebbor Gorge** has clearly been a waterfall. The stream now runs underground and there are some cave entrances below the gorge.

⑤ A small path runs along the tops of three fields with a long view across the Levels away to your left. With a stile on the right and a gate and horse trough in front, turn downhill with the fence on your right; follow the fence to a stile leading into the **Ebbor Gorge Nature Reserve**.

⑥ A second gate leads into a wood. At a junction with a red arrow and sign marked '**Car Park**' pointing forward, turn right into the valley and go down it – this narrows to an exciting, rocky gully. At the foot of the gorge turn right, signposted '**Car Park**'. You are now back at Point ② of the outward walk. After crossing a stream turn left at a T-junction to the wood edge, and back right to the car park.

WHERE TO EAT AND DRINK
The **Wookey Hole Inn** has real ale and a sculpture garden. The food is not cheap but it is home-cooked and unusual. There is also a family restaurant, the **Galloper**, in the large Wookey Hole visitor car park.

Wells and Ebbor Gorge

A walk of twice the length, taking in the gorge, and England's smallest city.
See map and information panel for Walk 38

•DISTANCE•	10 miles (16.1km)
•MINIMUM TIME•	4hrs 30min
•ASCENT / GRADIENT•	900ft (270m) ▲▲▲
•LEVEL OF DIFFICULTY•	🚶🚶 🚶🚶 🚶🚶
•PATHS•	Two wooded combes and a high hillside
•PARKING•	Pay-and-display on A371 on edge of Wells

Walk 39 Directions (Walk 38 option)

From the car park (Point Ⓐ) a path runs beside the **A371**, into **Wells**. Keep ahead into a narrow lane and at its end turn right ('**City Centre**'). Bear left into **Sadler Street**, where an arch on the left leads to the cathedral. Pass through the **Penniless Porch** to the market place, but at once take another arch into the **Bishop's Palace**. Turn right and go round two sides of the moat to emerge on to the busy **B3139**. Cross to a gateway on to **Tor Hill**, Point Ⓑ.

The path climbs up steps to emerge on to a strip of open grassland. Once under trees again, continue for 50yds (46m) to a stile on the left. Now in another open strip, follow a broken wall on the left to a stile. Go down through woodland to a stream. Turn right on a streamside path adjacent to rugby pitches. Beyond these it continues around the left side of a golf course to the **B3139**, Point Ⓒ. Cross to a gate signposted '**West Horrington**'. A path heads to the right, ascending **Biddle Combe**.

After 1½ miles (2.4km) a bridleway arrives from the right over a bridge, with a stream junction just above; here cross the left-hand stream and go up beside it. The path rises to the top of the wood to reach the A39, Point Ⓓ.

Cross to a stile. Bear right to join a fence, contouring round **Pen Hill** below the radio mast. Pass just outside one of the support cables to a stile. Walk round two sides of the next field to a similar stile. Continue ahead with a wall on your left to the **Old Bristol Road**, Point Ⓔ. Turn left, then right, into a track signposted '**Dursdon Drove**'. Bear left on the track marked 'Rookham View Private Road'. It bends right through farm buildings to a gate. Keep ahead, along the top of two fields, to a gate and a stile.

This is Point ⑤ on Walk 38. Continue to Point ⑥, down Ebbor Gorge, then round to Point ②. Carry on to Point ④, (Point Ⓕ of this walk). Now follow the **West Mendip Way** waymarkers: down the lane, with a short diversion into fields on the left. Where the lane bends left keep ahead on to a path – down into **Wells**, to cross the **A371** by the car park.

Walk 40

Cheddar Gorge

A circuit around Somerset's most impressive natural feature and beside the home of its gorgeous cheese.

•DISTANCE•	3½ miles (5.7km)
•MINIMUM TIME•	2hrs 15min
•ASCENT / GRADIENT•	1,000ft (300m) ▲▲▲
•LEVEL OF DIFFICULTY•	🚶 🚶 🚶
•PATHS•	Stony and sometimes steep and slippery, 3 stiles
•LANDSCAPE•	Crag tops and woods
•SUGGESTED MAP•	aqua3 OS Explorer 141 Cheddar Gorge
•START / FINISH•	Grid reference: ST 462536
•DOG FRIENDLINESS•	Open land, but care needed near cliff edges
•PARKING•	Pay-and-display at Cliff Street, close to visitor car park for Cheddar Gorge show caves
•PUBLIC TOILETS•	Toilets outside car park, and at showcaves

Walk 40 Directions

From the car park turn right, across a roundabout and over the river to the entrance to the gorge road. This looks more like a fairground than a public highway: indeed it has been a fairground since early Victorian times. Ignoring it for now, bear right into **Lippiatt** and go up this steep lane for 80yds (73m). Steps on the left lead up to another lane. Go up this to a signed footpath into some woods. At the top is a metal viewpoint tower: it gives a fine view into the gorge, and out to the sea, the distant Quantocks and the Exmoor coast.

A wide path runs uphill, close to the edge of the gorge. Steps arriving from the left are 'Jacob's Ladder', a Victorian attraction whereby visitors to the show caves paid to walk up on to a public footpath. After the steps the path is clear, but the well-trodden limestone becomes very slippery when it's damp. On the left are various viewpoints overlooking the gorge. Careful – King Edmund of England narrowly escaped falling over the edge when hunting up here in the year AD 941, and he wasn't the last.

At the highest point of the path ignore gates on the right but continue between fence and gorge. The path descends quite steeply through a wood to a stile. After a short level stretch it continues down through the wood – this can be muddy and slippery – to the gorge road.

A path ahead continues into the **Blackrock Nature Reserve**, but the **Gorge Walk** turns left down the roadside for 120yds (110m) to a waymarked path that climbs through the woods on the right.

> **WHERE TO EAT AND DRINK** ⓘ
> The gorge has many pubs and cafés, ranging from the cheap to the classy. Walkers may like the **White Hart**, which is a cavers' hang-out.

WHAT TO LOOK FOR ⓘ

In early summer you may find the **Cheddar pink**. This is a close relative of the garden pink and looks very like it – they are both *Dianthus*. Its single, fragrant flower grows out of cracks in the limestone around the gorge – and nowhere else in Britain.

After an initially steep ascent it turns left up a long flight of wood-and-earth steps. It continues with a fence on its right and the gorge on its left, gently downhill through thorn scrub that's adorned in autumn with old man's beard. The whiskery seed heads appear in autumn; in spring the flower is called travellers' joy.

At a junction a stile on the left is a side-path running down to the National Trust's (NT) viewpoint. This path descends steeply to an exposed slope above crags: a sensible sign suggests that dogs and children should be closely controlled, and the place should be avoided when very wet or by those with flat-soled shoes. It does give a fine outlook on the gorge mouth and the rockfaces opposite.

From the NT viewpoint return over the stile to the path junction and turn left. Head downhill now for 250yds (229m). Turn right, away from the gorge, at a low signpost marked '**Cheddar**'.

Cheddar is, of course, doubly famous, not only for its gorge but also for its cheese. Cheddar cheese does not have holes in (that's Emmental, from Switzerland) but Cheddar's holes did originally have cheese in: they were stored underground where the temperature is a chill-cabinet 4°C (39°F) all the year round. The particular process of 'cheddaring' consists of slicing up the curd at a crucial moment, placing it in layers and letting it slump – much the same as what's happened to the limestone strata overhead. The process is fairly easily reproduced on an industrial scale, so that we now have New Zealand Cheddar, Orkney Cheddar, and Cheddar from everywhere in between. However, authentic, hand-made Cheddar is available at Cheddar Gorge and is considerably tastier than the orange lumps vacuum wrapped in plastic found on supermarket shelves.

WHILE YOU'RE THERE ⓘ

The **Cheddar Caves and Gorge**, crowded as they are, are still impressive; try to visit before noon and on a weekday. Also interesting are the **Toy and Model Museum** and the **Cheddar Gorge Cheese Company**, where you can follow the cheese-making process.

Ignore a gate on the left but turn downhill at the first of two stiles. The path goes down under trees with a broken wall on its right, then passes through the wall at a kissing gate. At the first houses of Cheddar turn sharp left into a walled path. At the track below turn left to arrive among the shops and attractions of Cheddar Gorge near the tourist information centre.

Turn right, into a path forbidden to cyclists. It passes behind a **mill pool** and a slightly incongruous crazy golf course, then runs along the foot of a wood, with a rare chance for the observant to glimpse the extinct sabre-tooth tiger. Rejoin the main road through the gorge at the toilets, and head down past (or via) the tea rooms and snack shops to the car park.

Straight to the Parrett's Mouth

No cliffs or crashing waves – a coastal walk to heighten your understanding of flatlands and mud.

•DISTANCE•	4½ miles (7.2km)
•MINIMUM TIME•	1hr 45min
•ASCENT / GRADIENT•	Negligible
•LEVEL OF DIFFICULTY•	
•PATHS•	Town paths, wide, surfaced track and fields, 17 stiles
•LANDSCAPE•	Level ground, mudflats and sea
•SUGGESTED MAP•	aqua3 OS Explorer 153 Weston-super-Mare
•START / FINISH•	Grid reference: ST 305455
•DOG FRIENDLINESS•	Good, since half of walk is along open shoreline
•PARKING•	Street parking at Huntspill church
•PUBLIC TOILETS•	Just off-route in Highbridge

BACKGROUND TO THE WALK

The walk's start point was formerly several miles out to sea, with the shoreline at the foot of the Polden Hills (► Walk 20). Since the last Ice Age the tidal flow up and down the Bristol Channel has created the bank of clay mud on which you are now standing. Huntspill church, and the nearby houses, are built on Plymor Hill. At just 2ft (60cm) high, this must be the lowest hill in the country; even so, during the floods of 1981, the people who live here were glad of the extra altitude.

Managing Mud

Humans have drained the land behind this mud ridge to form the Somerset Levels and moors (► Walk 37). The watercourses that drain all that fertile 'summer land' – the Kings Sedgemoor Drain, the Parrett itself – would also let the sea back in at every high tide, and so they must be closed off. We shall pass the barrier that closes the River Brue in the course of the walk. On the left you pass a concrete pill box, a coastal defence from World War Two. On the other side, across the River Brue, you'll see a defence built against an enemy even more dangerous than the Germans: the sea itself. The Environment Agency, currently responsible for keeping the sea out of Britain, is coming to realise that such Canute-like and unsubtle ways of fighting the ocean are going to become less and less effective as global warming brings a rise in the sea, more autumn storms, and higher rainfall to swell the rivers behind. In November 2000 the Deputy Prime Minister, John Prescott, was very impressed by a Dutch system of overflow areas: deliberately letting floodwaters into certain areas for pumping out afterwards. 'Britain needs such a system' he declared – but in the Somerset Levels, Britain already has it.

Hinkley Point

On the other side of the estuary stands what is either a noble and striking focus for the rather flat landscape, or a sinister horror; which of the two you see depends largely on which newspaper you believe. Is the nuclear power station at Hinkley Point an environmental nightmare, spreading radioactive pollutants and threatening us all with cancer and worse? Or is it part of the only medium-term solution to carbon dioxide emissions and global warming? (My own suspicion is that it's probably both these things.) There's a certain irony in the fact that within its fence the Hinkley Point power station harbours a small nature reserve protecting the home of 29 different types of butterfly and the rare bee orchid, and is a haven for the nightingale as well.

Walk 41 Directions

① Head away from the church with houses on your right and trees on your left (with the sea somewhere behind them). The street, **Church Road**, bends right then back left: at the next bend keep ahead in **Longlands Lane**, which becomes a ditched track under poplars. Join a

concrete track that bends right to ugly **Maundril's Farm**.

② Turn left on a waymarked footpath between huge sheds. Cross a track to a stile, and turn half-right to cross a field to a footbridge. A fenced path leads to a street and continues beyond it. It passes along the end of a second street, to reach a third.

Walk 41

> **WHILE YOU'RE THERE** ⓘ
> **Coombes Somerset Cider**, at Japonica
> Farm in Mark village, is a commercial
> cider farm where you can watch the
> traditional cider-making process. You can
> also taste cider and perry – perry being
> similar to cider but made from pears.

> **WHERE TO EAT AND DRINK** ⓘ
> The **Crossways** is an old coaching inn
> with good food, real ales and
> considerable atmosphere. Dogs are
> accepted on leads and families are
> welcome. There is also the **Royal
> Artillery Arms** and, just over the bridge
> in Highbridge, the **Highbridge Inn**.

③ Again a tarred path continues opposite, to emerge into a field. A fenced-off way runs round the edge of the field to a stile. Continue along the right-hand edge of the field to a corner.

④ Here a walled way leads out to the right: take this if you wish to cross the bridge to visit **Highbridge**. Opposite the **Highbridge Inn** is a memento of the former seaport: a handsome Victorian warehouse in brick and stone. (Toilets are found by bearing left at the roundabout to a car park.) The main walk continues from Point ④ along the field edge near the **River Brue**, with its banks of brown mud, to reach the sea lock.

⑤ Bear left for 30yds (27m) to a stile, and follow a path on the flood bank alongside the tidal river. As the banking reaches the sea, a stile and gate on the right lead on to the concrete top of more sea defences.

⑥ Follow what is in effect a concrete track along the shoreline for a mile (1.6km). Where the concrete disappears under grass bear left to a gate, and cross the

earth barrier to a tarred lane. After 150yds (137m) this leaves the shore to pass a litter bin, burnt-out when I last saw it but hopefully replaced.

⑦ Cross a stile here, and head towards **Huntspill church** on a faint field path with a hedge and ditch on your left. Cross a footbridge on the left – here field boundaries are made of water rather than of stone or prickly bush. Turn right alongside the hedge to join a track. After 300yds (274m) watch out for a footbridge on the right. Turn left towards the church, then bear right towards a house with white gables, to find a narrow footbridge. Head straight towards the church over several stiles, to enter the churchyard through a kissing gate.

> **WHAT TO LOOK FOR** ⓘ
> Between the sea wall and the sea is salt pasture. Grass isn't the only plant that's
> managed to occupy this difficult niche, periodically submerged in salt water. **Marsh
> samphire** grows out of the perforated blocks of the sea wall. This low plant has fleshy
> leaves and spreading frothy flowers of greenish yellow. It used to be pickled and eaten
> with fish. Given the amount of human settlement around the Bristol Channel it would be
> unwise to gather it here.

Over Crook Peak and Wavering Down

A high-level ridge wander in the western Mendips over a lot of geology to Somerset's shapeliest summit.

•DISTANCE•	6 miles (9.7km)
•MINIMUM TIME•	3hrs
•ASCENT / GRADIENT•	900ft (270m) ▲▲▲
•LEVEL OF DIFFICULTY•	👫 👫 👫
•PATHS•	Field edges, then wide clear paths, 6 stiles
•LANDSCAPE•	Open, grassy hilltop and ridge, and a wood
•SUGGESTED MAP•	aqua3 OS Explorer 153 Weston-super-Mare
•START / FINISH•	Grid reference: ST 392550
•DOG FRIENDLINESS•	Off-lead, but be aware of horses in woods and on open hill
•PARKING•	On road between Cross and Bleadon, west of Compton Bishop; also street parking in Cross and on A38
•PUBLIC TOILETS•	None on route

BACKGROUND TO THE WALK

The rock which forms the Mendips, as well as the White Peak and the Yorkshire Dales, used to be known as the Mountain limestone. This name has sadly been abandoned – perhaps after complaints from the non-Mountain limestones of Everest, the Pyrenees and the Eiger… Now called Carboniferous limestone, it was laid down at a time when England was under water and drifting slowly north across the equator. The next rocks to form on top, as the Carboniferous sea became a swampy river-delta, were the coal measures. A thick layer of coal has in fact eroded off the top of the Mendips and, like the Pennines, the Mendips have a coal field next door.

Comfort Underfoot

In the Pennines the limestone is layered with waterproof gritstone so that dry ground alternates with peat bog. The Mendips are limestone all the way down. This gives a very enjoyable form of walking or (perhaps even better) horse-riding. The grass is cropped short by roe deer and rabbits, and bright in spring with lime-loving wild flowers. The sides drop away in hawthorn scrub and the mildest of craggy bits to a wide, fertile plain. The path along the ridge is fast and easy, and every 20 minutes it peeps down into another wooded hollow. The other side of Somerset, the Quantocks, are a different sort of limestone but give the same delightful walking. Sadly, the Quantocks and the Mendips are small in area. Furthermore, elsewhere in England, or even in the world, there isn't very much of this limestone downland at all.

Geological Crunches

Geologists believe that, oddly, this is the second time around for the Mendips. The continental collision nicknamed 'the Africa Crunch' folded the sea-bottom limestones into mountains of about Ben Nevis height (which isn't very high – Ben Nevis in its prime was

Everest height). The soft, coal-like stuff was eroded away and the Mendip Mountains wore down to their present shape in the early dinosaur age. Then Britain sank, and the mountain outlines disappeared under thousands of feet (up to 1,000m) of ocean sediments. The next event, 'the Alpine Crunch', lifted everything up again about 50 million years ago, and since then the topping has gradually worn away to reveal the limestone landscape underneath.

Twice Made

According to this theory, the limestone gorges around the Mendips have formed twice over. The first time, as wadis or desert valleys scoured by flash floods; the second time, under Ice Age conditions, with the underground waterways frozen. Thus contradictory geological noticeboards explain Burrington Combe (desert wadi) and Cheddar Gorge (Ice Age meltwaters). Given that limestone gorges don't have rivers, they ought not to occur even once; doing it twice, for two different reasons, is good going!

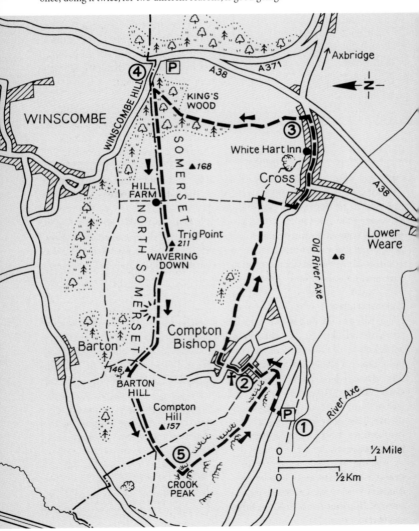

Walk 42 Directions

① Cross the road to a wide gate on the right (not the small gate ahead). A wide path contours round through brambly scrub, crosses the ridgeline and drops through a wood to its foot. Go down through a gate into **Compton Bishop** and turn left to the church.

WHILE YOU'RE THERE   ⓘ

King John's Hunting Lodge is a half-timbered house at the centre of Axbridge. Although King John granted this attractive old town its charter, he died about 300 years too early to take advantage of his supposed hunting lodge: the building is actually the house of a prosperous 16th-century merchant. It's now the town's free museum.

---

② The lane turns down, before the church, to a crossroads. Take the track opposite and follow it round a bend to its end. You will now contour round the base of the high slope of **Wavering Down**. Cross a stile, pass through a wrought-iron gate into a narrow paddock, and cross another stile into a large field; keep along the bottom edge of this. At its corner keep ahead over a stile, then through two gates, then move 40yds (37m) uphill around a fence corner to another stile on the same level. Follow the long bottom edge of a field to a track and turn right, down to the road. Turn left through **Cross** village.

③ At a 'Give Way 150yds' sign (warning of the A38 ahead) turn left up an enclosed path. It turns right above a fence, then slants up to rejoin the same fence higher up. It enters woodland, running above a bank of hornbeams: watch out for a waymarker where the path bears

right to pass through this bank. After a gate ignore a stile above to stay on the main track, which emerges at the top of the car park on **Winscombe Hill**.

④ Turn left, away from the car park, on a broad track, uphill. This rises through **King's Wood**, then dips slightly to pass the pantiled **Hill Farm**, before rising to the trig point on **Wavering Down**. Continue with a wall on your right, walking next to the wall for the sake of the views over it, to cross **Barton Hill**. In the dip below **Crook Peak** waymarkers point to left and right, but keep ahead to climb the slightly crag-topped summit.

⑤ Turn left and (with the small rocky drop down to your left) head down on to a long gentle ridge – outcrops of limestone poke out through the shallow grass of the path. At a railed barrier turn right on the path back to the car park.

WHERE TO EAT AND DRINK   ⓘ

The **White Hart** at Cross has undeniable atmosphere. Some of the Bloody Assizes were held here after the Battle of Sedgemoor (► Walk 20) and the inn is haunted by the ghost of one of Judge Jeffreys' victims. Rather more substantial is the inn's home-cooked food.

WHAT TO LOOK FOR   ⓘ

Limestone is made of **snails** – or at least of the calcareous hard parts of sea molluscs. Equally, snails are made of limestone, and flourish where calcium for shell-building is available. The shell is not only for protection from predators, but also keeps the snail from drying out. Accordingly, you are likely to see Crook Peak's snails in damp corners and on drizzly grey days. In these conditions you may be surprised at the brightness of snails – they are not just brown, but come in pinks and yellows as well.

Dolebury Warren

A fine walk through woodland, heathland and an Iron-Age hill fort on the northern rim of the Mendips.

•DISTANCE•	5¼ miles (8.4km)
•MINIMUM TIME•	2hrs 30min
•ASCENT / GRADIENT•	600ft (180m) ▲ ▲ ▲
•LEVEL OF DIFFICULTY•	🚶 🚶🚶 🚶🚶
•PATHS•	Wide and mostly mud-free, 4 stiles
•LANDSCAPE•	A grassy hilltop rises out of mixed woodland
•SUGGESTED MAP•	aqua3 OS Explorer 141 Cheddar Gorge
•START / FINISH•	Grid reference: ST 444575
•DOG FRIENDLINESS•	Dogs can run free in woods and on Dolebury Warren
•PARKING•	Pull-off near church; street parking around main Shipham crossroads
•PUBLIC TOILETS•	Burrington Combe on Walk 44

BACKGROUND TO THE WALK

Somerset has a lot of Iron-Age forts. It may just be that Somerset has rather a lot of the right sort of hill. These hill forts were not just defensive structures, but small townships. Inside the summit wall were roundhouses of wattle and daub. Wattle is a woven framework of willow twigs, and its daub is a mixture of clay and straw – the most waterproof daub also has plenty of cow-dung in it. Reed thatch made a cosy roof. The houses were up to 50ft (16m) across with a central fireplace.

'Barbarian' Propaganda

The inhabitants of these hill forts are the first people about whom we have written records. However, the writers were their enemies, the Romans. The Durotinges, who inhabited Somerset and Dorset, are portrayed, along with the other British tribes, as warlike and savage barbarians. Warlike would seem to be correct. Their settlements, whether hill forts or the lake village at Glastonbury, were placed so as to be defended. In the case of the hill forts, they clearly valued the protective wall above having a convenient water supply. And Boudica, often called Boadicea, chieftain of the Iceni of East Anglia, certainly earned the respect of the Romans even though they eventually defeated her, as they did the Durotinges on Cadbury Castle. 'Savage barbarians', however, is just enemy propaganda.

These were people with a developed civilisation based on farming, fishing and hunting, as well as warfare. At Glastonbury their village on stilts in the marshland is itself a considerable feat of co-operative working from a very early time. They built log trackways across the peatlands, or paddled home in a canoe hollowed out of a single tree trunk with flint axes and fire.

Iron Age Craft and Culture

They traded with their neighbours; rounded pebbles from Chesil Beach, used as ammunition by slingers, have been found at Ham Hill. They wove baskets and made jewellery of bronze. They appreciated fine, or at least garish, clothing, coloured using plant dyes (madder for red and woad for blue) and pinned with a bronze brooch at the shoulder. They kept bees, and they made pottery which is still an inspiration to potters of today. At night the roundhouse was lit with rushlights made from the pith of reeds and soaked in mutton fat. And from what we know of Iron Age-type societies in more recent history, they had a rich tradition of story-telling and a detailed knowledge of their own family trees.

Walk 43 Directions

① From the main crossroads in the centre of **Shipham** village head uphill on **Hollow Road** (signposted for '**Rowberrow**'). At the top of the

street bear right into **Barn Pool**, then turn right again into **Lipiatt Lane**. Continue walking up the hill, then at its end keep going straight ahead on a path with a waymarker for **Cheddar**, to descend a sunken path to a stream.

② Just before the stream turn left on a path marked '**Rowberrow**'. Stay to the left of the stream (ignoring a fork to the right) – the path becomes a tarred track. After passing three houses and a limekiln bear right into the forest at a noticeboard, '**Rowberrow Warren**'.

③ The track bends to the right, climbing. At the corner of an open field turn left into a smaller track that descends gently with this field above on its right. At a junction keep ahead, uphill, for 35yds (32m) then turn left on a forest track with a bridleway sign.

> **WHILE YOU'RE THERE** ⓘ
> For a complete change from the tranquil Mendips, there's the **Helicopter Museum** at Weston-super-Mare. The world's oldest, fastest and ugliest helicopters; and, once a month, open cockpit days and even flying lessons.

④ After 350yds (320m) this track ends; bear left down a wide path with clear-felled forest above on the right. Where it joins a stony track and path below, bear right on the stony track, with a wall to your left. At a T-junction turn left for 90yds (82m) to a gate on the left with a National Trust sign.

⑤ Follow the grassy ridgeline ahead, passing along the left side of a fenced enclosure of scrubland. At its end, bear right ('**Limestone Link**' waymarker) to pass to the right of a tall pine clump. Emerge

> **WHERE TO EAT AND DRINK** ⓘ
> The **Miners' Arms** at Shipham serves real ales and bar meals. Dogs are welcome at the outdoor seating area; children are allowed indoors as well. There is also the **Star** (at Star!), just before the end of the walk.

> **WHAT TO LOOK FOR** ⓘ
> **Gruffy ground**: on the final ascent from Star to Shipham you pass among many small hollows. These are the remains of mines. Most of the Mendip mines were for lead, but the ones here were for calamine, an ore containing zinc. A miner would dig a small hole, stand in it, and throw his hack (or pick-axe) as far as possible in all directions. Where it landed was the edge of his claim.

on to more open grassland with wide views. The highest point of the ridge is the rim of the huge **Dolebury hill fort**.

⑥ A green track runs down through the fort and into the woods below. It bends left, then back right, to emerge at a gate on to tarred lanes. Take the lane on the right, down to the **A38**. Cross to a signposted bridleway: this leafy path with a bedrock bottom rises to a lane. Turn left – the hummocky ground on the left consists of broken stones from the disused **Churchill Quarry** below. Ignore turnings to left and right and follow the enclosed track down to **Star**.

⑦ Cross the **A38** on to a grass track to a stile, and go up the grassy spur above. Keep to the left of some trees to a stile, and pass to the right of a football pitch, to find a short path out to the edge of **Shipham**. Turn right, to the village centre.

Batch and Combe

A longer and more demanding option, to the summit of the Mendips.
See map and information panel for Walk 43

•DISTANCE•	8½ miles (13.7km)
•MINIMUM TIME•	4hrs 30min
•ASCENT / GRADIENT•	1,500ft (450m) ▲▲▲
•LEVEL OF DIFFICULTY•	👥 👥 👥

Walk 44 Directions
(Walk 43 option)

The cap of sandstone that lies on the Mendip limestone means that Beacon Batch is more like Exmoor or the Pennines, with gorse, heather and peat. Burrington Combe was formed as a rainwater gulch in hot desert conditions, and is still much drier than Beacon Batch.

At Point Ⓐ (Point ② of Walk 43) cross the stream and turn right on a bridleway that gradually rises up the left-hand side of its little valley to **Tynings Farm**. After the buildings turn left on a field track to the heathland of Beacon Batch. Ignoring bridleway waymarkers, turn right on a path that slants gradually up to join a much larger one for the final 350yds (320m) to the summit trig point, Point Ⓑ.

Bear left (second exit, in roundabout terms) on a descending path that joins another to slant down to the right. At the corner of the open heath turn towards the **B3134** and follow it down to a small car park, Point Ⓒ.

Take the rocky bridleway just above the road. After 200yds (183m) a footpath turns off left along the crest of **Burrington Ham**. After ½ mile (800m) this bends left: here take a small, waymarked path to reach a rocky outcrop, Point Ⓓ.

Turn right below the outcrop on a slanting path down into woods. Where it levels off, turn sharp left to join a bridleway. This becomes a lane: keep ahead where a steeper lane descends to the right, to reach the **B3134** at Link. Turn left alongside the road to pass the **Burrington Inn** and admire **Burrington Combe** and the **Rock of Ages**, Point Ⓔ, where the Revd John Toplady sheltered from a thunderstorm in a cleft that looks barely waterproof and subsequently wrote the famous hymn. (He didn't find the drier and deeper Plumley's Den, near by, but 'Den of Ages' isn't nearly as good a hymn title.)

Return along the **B3134**, bearing left into a track and turning up left on a short but steep path. Turn left in the lane above, which becomes a track with a parking area. After 200yds (183m) fork left. Follow the main track round to the right into a valley, with conifers rising on its left. Where the bridleways divide, fork right for 90yds (82m) to a gate on the left with a National Trust sign – this is Point ⑤ on Walk 43.

Through Geological Time in the Avon Gorge

A fascinating walk through a famous gorge with a chance to see one of Brunel's masterpieces.

•DISTANCE•	4¼ miles (6.8km)
•MINIMUM TIME•	2hrs
•ASCENT / GRADIENT•	350ft (110m) ▲ ▲ ▲
•LEVEL OF DIFFICULTY•	🚶 🚶 🚶
•PATHS•	Wide and waymarked, one steep section, no stiles
•LANDSCAPE•	Wooded slopes, tidal riverside, and a gorge
•SUGGESTED MAP•	aqua3 OS Explorer 154 Bristol West & Portishead
•START / FINISH•	Grid reference: ST 553740
•DOG FRIENDLINESS•	Dogs can be off leads throughout
•PARKING•	At Leigh Woods
•PUBLIC TOILETS•	Across Clifton Bridge, near observatory

Walk 45 **Directions**

A noticeboard near the car park shows two waymarked trails, one of which, the Purple Trail, is being upgraded to wheelchair-friendly smoothness. This walk links parts of the two trails with the riverside walk along the famous gorge.

Start from the noticeboard on the **Red Trail**. This begins as a wide gravel path towards the river. After 50yds (46m) a sculpture on the left has been chain-sawn out of a tree: it portrays a mattock, a tool for hacking the ground. Here the trail bears right. In another 90yds (82m) turn left on the **Red Trail** as the Purple Trail continues ahead.

The wide path runs under beech trees, past a shelter that is roofed with shingles (wooden tiles). At a T-junction, with a bench, the trail turns left, heading up along the rim of a wooded combe. It bears right,

into the combe, and turns along its floor for 200yds (183m). The trail then turns left on to a terrace path with glimpses of the river below. The sound that could be the roar of the Avon's rapids is in fact the traffic on the A4 on the far bank.

After 300yds (274m), at a point with a view ahead along the river, the **Red Trail** bears right on a smaller path past a picnic table. It slants down across a shallow combe

WHAT TO LOOK FOR ℹ️

On the inland side of the riverside path you can spot 18th-century mooring bollards of the **Society of Merchant Venturers**. Bristol superseded Bridgwater as the most convenient safe harbour on the West England coastline, and so became Britain's second city. If you wanted raisins or sugar in the 17th century, you sent to Bristol for them. A well-maintained ship is 'Bristol fashion' and a leading brand of sherry appears to come from Bristol rather than Spain. The port was also a centre of the slave trade.

> **WHERE TO EAT AND DRINK** ⓘ
> The **George Inn** at Abbot's Leigh has a family garden, and serves food and traditional ales.

and reaches a T-junction. Here, where the Red Trail turns uphill, turn down, following blue markers. These indicate a cycle trail. At its foot is the **River Avon**, where you turn right – your route now follows the Avon upstream on a wide riverside path for 1½ miles (2.4km).

The river possibly predates the low hills it runs through. The land was pushed up into a dome as a distant effect of continental movements elsewhere: Africa banging against Spain 300 million years ago. As the land rose the river carved its way down to form the gorge. The doming caused by the 'Africa Crunch' can be seen in the cliff faces opposite. The left-hand crags are reddish sandstone of Devonian age, some of the oldest rocks in Somerset. These have also been used in the railway wall alongside your path. Upstream, you pass opposite a high wall of pale brown limestone, its strata dipping steeply to the right. As we head upstream, we are also passing forward through the geological ages, passing from the Devonian to the Carboniferous roughly 50 million years later.

But geological studies are distracted by the impressive Clifton Bridge, now almost overhead. Some 130yds (118m) before the bridge a rock-buttress opposite is studded with metal pins to stop it falling on the A4. Here turn off to the right, passing under a railway bridge numbered 19. A small and rather rough path goes up the floor of **Nightingale Valley**. Here you may

feel with your feet a practical consequence of shifting from the Devonian to the Carboniferous: the limestone bedrock forms a particularly sticky sort of mud.

At the valley top a kissing gate ahead leads out on to a street; a left turn in this street would take you out on to the **Clifton Bridge** (¾ mile, 1.2km). Alternatively, the **Blue Trail** on the right can provide a quick return (¾ mile, 1.2km) to the car park. However, our route turns sharp right before the gate, on to a path marked 'No Bikes'. This runs alongside the drop into **Nightingale Valley** on the right. It passes through the earthworks of **Stokeleigh Camp**, to reach a viewpoint overlooking the river.

From this viewpoint turn sharp left, alongside wooden railings protecting the drop on the right. After 250yds (229m) the path forks: bear right, to pass through the earthwork to a small pond on the left. Turn left, with the ditch and earth wall of the hill fort on your left. After 200yds (183m) a **Purple Trail** waymarker points to the right. The trail, recently resurfaced in yellowish gravel, is unmistakable even without the waymarkers as it leads through the woods. It arrives at the tarred access track with speed bumps, close to the car park.

> **WHILE YOU'RE THERE** ⓘ
> A short diversion – 2 miles (3.2km) out and back – will take you on to the **Clifton Bridge** itself, and across it to the Clifton Bridge Museum. Here you can see pictures, models and explanations of the bridge's construction. If this fires you with enthusiasm for I K Brunel – as well it may – you could visit the SS *Great Britain* and Temple Meads Station, both in Bristol city centre.

Goblin Combe and Corporation Woods

A forest full of rockfaces gives a walk of crag tops and hollows.

•DISTANCE•	5¼ miles (8.4km)
•MINIMUM TIME•	2hrs 20min
•ASCENT / GRADIENT•	400ft (210m) ▲ ▲ ▲
•LEVEL OF DIFFICULTY•	🚶 🚶 🚶
•PATHS•	Tracks and paths, one steep-stepped ascent, 3 stiles
•LANDSCAPE•	Wooded hollows and open pasture above
•SUGGESTED MAP•	aqua3 OS Explorer 154 Bristol West & Portishead
•START / FINISH•	Grid reference: ST 459653
•DOG FRIENDLINESS•	Freedom in Cleeve Woods but leads essential in Corporation Wood (vermin traps)
•PARKING•	Goblin Combe car park (free) at Cleeve Hill Road (turn off A370 at Lord Nelson pub)
•PUBLIC TOILETS•	None on route

BACKGROUND TO THE WALK

Walkers in the Lake District or Wales become familiar with the effects of glaciers on the landscape: U-shaped valleys, corrie hollows, spurs with their bottom ends chopped away, and so on. Glaciers never reached Somerset, but the county has certain so-called 'peri-glacial' landforms, caused by the permafrosted tundra climate just next door to the ice cap. Where, for example, is the fair-sized river that carved out the rocky Goblin Combe?

This is limestone country, and the water flows under the ground. But in the Ice Age times the underground was frozen, and the summer meltwaters could flow across the surface and make gorges. Ice Age freeze-and-thaw action in the rocks has broken off large boulders, which lie on either side of the track, and smaller pieces which form scree at the crag foot.

'Adventure Climbing'

Goblin Combe's rocks provide short but entertaining climbs. Notices forbidding climbing are to some extent a legal fiction. The law as it stands doesn't understand the self-reliant ethos of rock-climbing; and the landowner could, in theory, be sued by a fallen climber. Nevertheless, venturing on to the rocks without the proper skill and equipment is both stupid and dangerous. Unlike many limestone cliffs in Somerset you will not – or at least should not – see bolt anchors drilled into Goblin's rocks. Rock climbers and the British Mountaineering Council have designated this an 'adventure climbing' area, where such aids to easier and safer climbing are not seen as sporting.

Limestone Heath Paradox

Above the crags and treetops is limestone meadow with many wild flowers. Here is also limestone heath – a paradox to gardeners, who know that heathers hate lime. Once again, the answer lies in the Ice Age, when acidic, sandy soil from elsewhere blew in on the subzero winds. Sadly, the airy openness of the crag-top meadow is spoilt by the procession of aircraft taking off from Bristol International Airport.

Most of the woodland in Goblin Combe is of ash trees – typical in the Mendips, but relatively rare in Britain as a whole, where the natural succession arrives at oak, birch or (in the mountains) Scots pine. The ash, however, wins out over its rivals on this thin limestone soil. Later in the walk, Corporation Wood is of beeches. Climax woodland (that is a wood that has no further tendency to evolve into some other sort of wood) is composed of a tree species that throws sufficient shade to suppress others. Beeches are particularly good at this, and so Corporation Wood is open and spacious between the smooth tree trunks. Below, there's an occasional 'etiolated' (made pale for want of light) evergreen such as holly, yew or ivy. Also, of course, the young seedlings of the beech wood itself, specially adapted to the heavy shade of their parents.

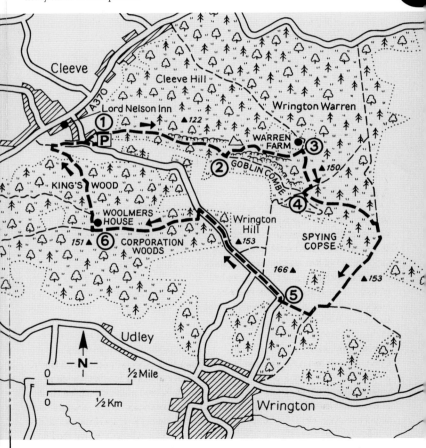

Walk 46 Directions

① From the parking area turn right into **Plunder Street** and bear left past the **Goblin Combe**

Environmental Centre to pass through a gateway marked 'Footpath to Wrington only'. An earth track leads up the combe bottom, with grey crags above on the left.

Walk 46

② After ¾ mile (1.2km) the track passes through a wall gap. Here, beside a map of permissive paths, turn up the one on the left. Steep steps lead up to the top of the slope, where the small path turns right alongside a broken wall. On the right, yew trees conceal the drop beyond, but after 100yds (91m) the path bears right to reach the open crag top. Turn left for 270yds (247m) into a clearing. After another 100yds (91m) is a barrier with a stile. A green track leads down to a noticeboard near outbuildings of **Warren Farm**. (The noticeboard indicates 'You are here' but actually you're slightly further to the south…)

③ Turn right on a green track; it goes gently uphill at first, then descends and bears left to the floor of a wooded combe. Turn right for 110yds (100m) to a junction of combes and tracks.

④ Turn sharp left, past tree trunk obstructions, on a green track in the bottom of a new combe. With the wood edge visible ahead, bear left to a barrier and turn right in the track beyond. This runs along the wood edge. Sudden loud noises here may be jays in the wood (or aeroplanes taking off!). After the corner of **Spying Copse** the track runs into open pasture. It turns right and

WHERE TO EAT AND DRINK ⓘ
The **Lord Nelson**, on the A370, could be described as a 'cheap steak' inn; but it does have a pleasant beer garden and an indoor play area for children.

then left, and after another 100yds (91m) watch out for a kissing gate on the right-hand side: a grassy way leads across a field to a lane (**Wrington Hill**).

⑤ Turn right for ¾ mile (1.2km), and, as the road leaves the beeches of **Corporation Woods**, turn back left on a track following the signpost marked 'Congresbury Woodlands'. The house on the left has a commendable attempt at topiary (tree-clipping) in bay leaves. After a bungalow on the right-hand side the track descends to **Woolmers House**.

WHILE YOU'RE THERE ⓘ
Nearby **Clevedon** is an elegant seaside resort. Its Victorian pier is one of the finest surviving and is 1,100ft (335m) long. If you time it correctly you can step from the pier on to the paddle steamers, *Waverley* or *Balmoral*, for a trip to the new Severn Bridge.

⑥ After passing the kennels, turn right on a waymarked track, to go through two gates into **King's Wood**. The broad path ahead leads to a waymarked footbridge. After another 50yds (46m) bear left with the waymarkers. The path runs down to a stile at the foot of the wood. Bear slightly left towards a gap in the trees and a gate, but turn right along the foot of the field. A stile on the left leads to a tarred lane and the car park.

WHAT TO LOOK FOR ⓘ
The rare **moonwort fern** grows under the yew trees of Goblin Combe. Its ragged-looking fronds are 2–8 inches (5–20cm) long with brown spore structures rather like dry seed heads. Alchemists believed this fern would help them turn mercury into silver.

Hunstrete and Compton Dando

Serenity enjoyed in a rich landscape nestling between the busy cities of Bristol and Bath.

•DISTANCE•	6¼ miles (10.1km)
•MINIMUM TIME•	3hrs 30min
•ASCENT / GRADIENT•	700ft (210m)
•LEVEL OF DIFFICULTY•	
•PATHS•	Tracks, field paths, woodland paths, and byways, 15 stiles
•LANDSCAPE•	Rolling farmland with plantations and small streams
•SUGGESTED MAP•	aqua3 OS Explorer 155 Bristol & Bath
•START / FINISH•	Grid reference: ST 632644
•DOG FRIENDLINESS•	Some freedom in woods and on tracks fenced off from farmland
•PARKING•	Street parking near bridge in Woollard; also opposite pub in Compton Dando (Point ⑥)
•PUBLIC TOILETS•	None on route

BACKGROUND TO THE WALK

Somerset as an entity is older than England itself; it came into existence as a kingdom of the Saxons after their defeat of King Arthur. This book conforms to the ancient boundaries established, perhaps by Alfred himself, in the 9th century. Local Government reorganisation in 1974 split off a section and called it 'Avon' – the people of Somerset were not pleased. Destruction-of-Somerset Day happened to be 1st April, and to mark this particular All Fools' Day a muffled quarter-peal of *Somerset Surprise Major* was rung from Yatton church.

Name Game

Local government re-reorganisation in 1996 largely restored the ancient county. However, this corner remains separate as a unitary authority called Bath and North East Somerset, resulting in the unfortunate acronym, 'BANES'. The other end of Avon has become another unitary authority, North Somerset. The very names of them are an admission that they may be convenient units of government but aren't actually proper places at all. Although it has no striking natural features, 'BANES' does have a character of its own. It can be seen as the final petering-out of the Cotswolds, even if it does lack the Cotswolds' sudden edges – for the most part it's a quiet land of gentle hills, with villages hidden in the occasional small valley. It's rich farming country, with small but bushy woods on the slopes and stream banks too steep for the plough.

Bigoted Views

A remnant of that farming wealth is at Hunstrete, where there's an attractive little angling lake that makes a good picnic spot. It was one of six dug into the grounds of Hunstrete House – a magnificent country mansion of 17 bays with statues to match. It was planned in the 1780s under the influence of Bath's new streets and squares, incomplete in 1797 and already falling down in 1822. Landscaping plans at nearby country houses were even more ambitious and expensive. At Marston Bigot and at Berkley, to improve the view from the windows, they removed and rebuilt a parish church. The authorities charged with making up reasons for footpaths have had to use some imagination. At the start of this walk you'll use the Two Rivers Way: the rivers are Yeo and Chew. From Lord's Wood to Hunstrete you're on the 'Three Peaks Way': these are not Ben Nevis, Snowdon and Scafell Pike; they aren't even Yorkshire's Whernside, Pen-y-ghent and Ingleborough. They are, in fact, Maes Knoll, Knowle Hill and Blackberry Hill, but none of this will detract from the pleasure of this walk. Towards its end you'll come across a relic of the real Somerset: a few hummocks here are the Wansdyke, possibly a defensive wall of the Britons, laid out even at Arthur's command, against the Saxon invaders.

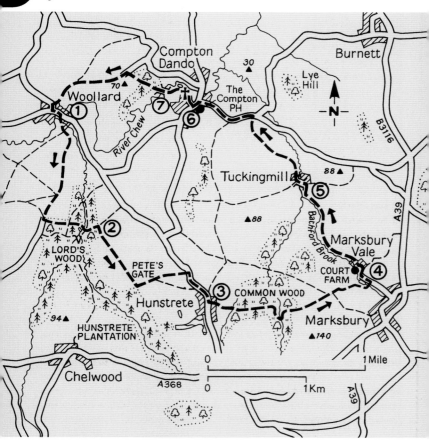

Walk 47 Directions

① At the southern end of **Woollard** bear right at a 'Circular Walk' sign. The byway is underwater at first,

but a path parallels it on the right. After the byway becomes **Birchwood Lane**, turn left into **Lord's Wood**, on a path waymarked '**Three Peaks Way**'. Go downhill, crossing a track, to a pool. Pass

Walk 47

WHAT TO LOOK FOR ⓘ

The **weather-vane** at Compton Dando looks rather like a dragon and is, locals say, the Dando itself. The inscription on the lychgate, referring to its function as a shelter for coffins, states 'Resurgam' – I shall rise again.

around to the left of this, to a waymarker and a track junction. The track opposite leads up to the edge of the wood.

② Turn right, and drop to a hidden footbridge under trees. Head uphill, passing the right-hand edge of a plantation, to **Pete's Gate** beside a corner of **Hunstrete Plantation**. Turn left to a field gate. Now the right of way bears right, but, with no sign of a path, it's simpler to keep ahead to a lane and turn right into **Hunstrete**.

③ Turn left beside **Cottage No 5**. Ignoring the waymarking arrow, go down the right-hand side of a field to a stile into **Common Wood**. The track ahead passes through a paintball sports area. Where it crosses a stream and bends left, take a waymarked green path that rises to the top of the wood. Pass through a small col with a lone ash tree, down to a hedge corner. Go straight downhill to a signpost, and turn right to join a lane at **Marksbury Vale**.

④ Turn left towards **Court Farm**; just before the buildings turn right over a stile, and take the right-hand

track for 100yds (91m) to a stile. Pass to the right-hand side of the farm buildings to an enclosed track following **Bathford Brook**. Head downstream to reach a track at **Tuckingmill**.

⑤ Follow the track past a handsome, 18th-century manor house to a ford. Cross the footbridge and turn right, alongside the stream, which is again the line of an underwater byway – rejoin it as it emerges. It leads to a road, with **Compton Dando** 700yds (640m) away on the left.

WHERE TO EAT AND DRINK ⓘ

The **Compton**, at Compton Dando, falls conveniently near the end of the walk and offers picnic tables, Bass beer and food. Well-behaved dogs are welcome; large parties (of people) are asked to phone beforehand. At Woollard, **Ye Olde Bell Farm** really is as old as its name pretends, and sells soft drinks.

⑥ Turn right into **Church Lane**, and then go through the lychgate. A stile leads down steps, one of which is a 17th-century gravestone. Turn left behind the mill house and pass to the left of the mill pond, to reach a footbridge over the **River Chew**.

⑦ Bear left into woodland known as **Park Copse**. At its top follow the right-hand edge of a field round to a stile. In the lane beyond turn left; it becomes a hedged track and runs alongside a tiny gorge as it descends to **Woollard**.

WHILE YOU'RE THERE ⓘ

The three impressive stone circles at **Stanton Drew** are only behind Avebury and Stonehenge in size and significance. Archaeologists assign them to the Bronze Age but legend offers a better explanation. Dancing at a wedding continued until the hour struck midnight. The fiddler then laid down his bow. 'No more,' he said; 'it is now the Sabbath.' But at that moment a mysterious figure stepped forward: 'I will play for your dancing.' It was, of course, Satan himself, and the dancers in their stony forms are dancing still...

Into the Hollows Around Wellow

A green valley walk, where Cotswold melds into Mendip, tracing a legacy of abandoned industry and failed technology.

•DISTANCE•	6½ miles (10.4km)
•MINIMUM TIME•	3hrs 30min
•ASCENT / GRADIENT•	984ft (300m) ▲▲▲
•LEVEL OF DIFFICULTY•	👫 👫 👫
•PATHS•	Byways, stream sides and some field paths, 12 stiles
•LANDSCAPE•	Grassy hillsides and valleys
•SUGGESTED MAP•	aqua3 OS Explorer 142 Shepton Mallet
•START / FINISH•	Grid reference: ST 739583
•DOG FRIENDLINESS•	Mostly pasture
•PARKING•	Street parking in village centre, or large car park below Peasedown road
•PUBLIC TOILETS•	None on route

BACKGROUND TO THE WALK

When you walk through this quiet corner of Somerset, it certainly doesn't strike you as an industrial landscape. You may, for example, wonder why such a sleepy valley ever needed its own railway. As you climb out of the Wellow Valley you might notice some odd conical hills. And then, at Combe Hay, with its lovely medieval manor house, there is some very peculiar 18th-century brickwork. Combe Hay and Wellow were actually at the heart of Somerset's industrial revolution. And the last coal mine here only closed in the 1970s.

Roman Coal Field

Like so much in Somerset, it started with the Romans. In the Temple of Minerva in nearby Bath, a fire burned – according to some historians, a living coal fire. Certainly by the 16th century the mines were going down. Squashed between the Mendips and the Cotswolds, the Somerset coal field is small and awkward. Many of the veins are vertical, and only a few feet (a metre or so) in width. So coal might be hacked from overhead, on an improvised platform jammed across a narrow shaft. And always, for miner and mine owner alike, there was the threat of cheaper and easier coal coming up the River Avon from Wales.

Canal and Caisson

This brings us to the engineering bricks in the field at Combe Hay. To move 100,000 tons of coal a year to Bath a canal was constructed that was ambitious even by the standards of the enterprising 18th century. Over its length of just 10 miles (16km), from Paulton Basin to Bath, the Somersetshire Coal Canal had two aqueducts and a tunnel. Furthermore, there was the problem of the 165ft (50m) climb on to Combe Hay Hill. The solution was, in effect, an underwater elevator. A barge on the upper canal entered a floating metal box called a caisson. The caisson was sealed, and water pumped in until it started to sink. It sank for 50ft (15m) to the bottom of the shaft. Its door was then matched up to a door in the base of the shaft; both doors were opened; and the barge floated out. The process would take seven minutes, unless the caisson got stuck. The ground around the caisson shaft is fuller's earth, which expands when wetted, and this may have caused the sides of the shaft to bulge inwards. The caissons were abandoned after only two years and replaced with an inclined plane. The southern branch of the canal, through Wellow to Radstock, was never completed. Instead, a horse-drawn tramway carried the coal out. Both canal and tramway were replaced by the railway, which in its turn has been superseded by motor roads.

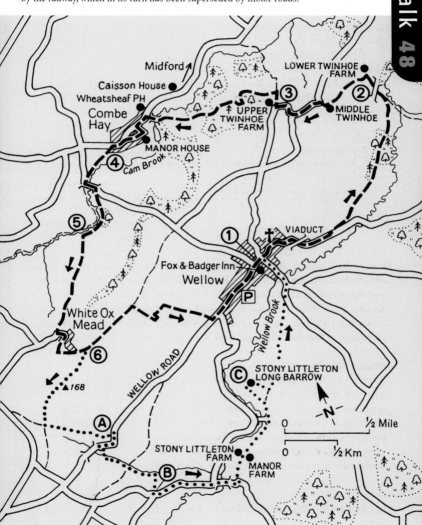

Walk 48 Directions

① Head out past the church and under a viaduct. Immediately after

Wellow Trekking a track starts just above the road. Where it becomes unclear, cross to the hedge opposite and continue above it. A new track runs through a wood, then down to the valley floor. Where a bridleway sign points right, turn left to pass under a railway bridge.

② Just before **Lower Twinhoe Farm** turn left into a signposted green track. At the hilltop the track fades into thistly ground. Bear right, before **Middle Twinhoe**, to a small gate. Turn right along the farm's driveway to a lane. Turn left, then to the right around farm buildings and bend left towards **Upper Twinhoe**. Just before this farm a signed track descends to the right.

> ### WHERE TO EAT AND DRINK
> The **Fox and Badger** is at the walk's start. The **Wheatsheaf** at Combe Hay is a handsome old building with a flowery terrace; it serves real ales and good food. Children are allowed in the dining area, and well-behaved dogs are welcome.

③ After 130yds (118m) turn left through a double gate and along a field top. The path then slants down through scrubby woodland towards **Combe Hay**. From the wood edge follow the lower edge of a field to a stone bridge into the village. Follow the main road left, to pass the **Manor House**.

④ After the last house of Combe Hay, find a gap in the wall on the left. Bear right, down to the **Cam Brook**, and follow it to a road bridge. Cross it and continue with the stream down on your right through a field and a wood. Follow the stream along another field to a stile, then along the foot of a short field to a gateway.

⑤ Don't go through this gateway, but turn up the field edge to a stile on the right instead. Slant up left across the next field to a nettly way between high thorns. At the top of

> ### WHAT TO LOOK FOR
> In all but the driest of conditions, the ascent towards White Ox Mead features some of the stickiest mud anywhere. The reason is **fuller's earth**: this is the special sort of clay (aluminium silicate) that was mined and used to wash wool with – as well as grease, it also absorbs water. The consequent swelling is what caused the caisson shaft at Combe Hay to bulge inwards and jam.

this bear right in a rutted track to a lane. Turn uphill to **White Ox Mead**, and follow the lane for another 60yds (55m) to a stile. Slant up to another stile, and turn up a tarred track to where it divides near a shed without walls.

⑥ Keep ahead on a rutted track along the hill crest. Ignore a waymarked stile to pass under low- and high-voltage electric cables. Here a small metal gate on the right leads to a hoof-printed path down beside a fence. At the foot of the field turn left, then left again (uphill), round a corner to a gate. Turn left across the field top and down its edge to the street leading into **Wellow**.

> ### WHILE YOU'RE THERE
> **Radstock Museum** gives much of its space to the coal industry. It has a reconstructed mine tunnel and items from that most attractive of ages (to look at afterwards if not to live through), the industrial 18th century.